THE DISADVANTAGED AND
LIBRARY EFFECTIVENESS

THE DISADVANTAGED AND LIBRARY EFFECTIVENESS

by Claire K. Lipsman
Formerly Senior Associate
Planning Research Corporation

American Library Association
Chicago 1972

Library of Congress Cataloging in Publication Data

Lipsman, Claire K
    The disadvantaged and library effectiveness.

    1. Libraries and the socially handicapped—United
States. I. Title.
Z711.92.S6L56   027.6'6   72-1375
ISBN 0-8389-0129-8

*This work was developed under a contract with the
U.S. Office of Education, Department of Health, Education
and Welfare. However, the opinions expressed herein
do not necessarily reflect the policy of that Agency,
and no official endorsement should be inferred.*

International Standard Book Number 0-8389-0129-8 (1972)

Library of Congress Catalog Card Number 72-1375

Manufactured in the United States of America

Contents

FIGURES

TABLES

APPENDIX TABLES

Preface

THE PUBLIC library is an important element in the complex of educational institutions serving the public. In the past it has played a vital role as a vehicle for social and economic mobility, as well as for intellectual development, by making available the means of self-education. Today public libraries, together with other educational institutions, face the difficult problem of filling this role for groups of disadvantaged persons whose needs and constraints appear to differ considerably from those of traditional library patrons.

Public libraries in urban areas are particularly oppressed by this problem and the need to find viable solutions. A major source of uncertainty and concern for those involved in library policy making is the extent to which programs and approaches to this problem should depart from traditional methods and techniques. A number of demonstration programs to serve the disadvantaged have been mounted, the majority with the assistance of federal funds. Since 1964 approximately $10 million of Title I Library Services and Construction Act funds has been expended in support of library services to the disadvantaged, in addition to many millions more of state and local funds. Some evaluation efforts have been made, but, in general, information and understanding that would lead to more effective program development and improved allocation of resources have been lacking. Existing measures of program impact and effectiveness are fragmentary, and few libraries have considered their services and role in relation to other community resources or to community needs.

vii

This is the context in which this study has been undertaken. It did not appear that the state of the art was such that a formal evaluation effort would be productive. The U.S. Office of Education therefore requested a study which would illuminate the problems of library service in urban low-income areas by examining a cross section of program approaches, target groups, and scopes of effort. This report is not to be considered an evaluation, but rather a pilot exploration of alternative approaches for reaching desired goals.

The report is concerned with the social utility of libraries and with the factors that appear to be requirements for effective programs. In the absence of established standards or criteria for measuring program effectiveness, we have substituted a comparative analysis of a number of programs based on detailed observation of the program process; a survey of needs and interests of the target groups, both users and nonusers; and an assessment of the library's role in the target neighborhood as it is perceived by other community institutions serving the same groups. Thus a basis for comparisons and for judgments has been introduced which provides a foundation for suggestions as to the direction in which programs of service to the disadvantaged might move.

To achieve the study objectives, library programs and practices in low-income neighborhoods were examined in a number of cities. In each of fifteen cities data were collected through interview and observation in four subject areas: (1) the needs and interests of the community residents, (2) library services in relation to other available community resources, (3) the nature and scope of the neighborhood library program and its relation to the rest of the library system, and (4) available measures of the impact or effectiveness of the program.

This report presents findings which, it is hoped, will be useful to those both within and without the library community who are concerned with the future of the library as an institution with a social function. Taken together, these findings imply the need for substantial changes in concept if libraries are to meet the functional service needs of the disadvantaged. Currently the value of the urban public library for meeting these needs is open to serious question. Both the medium and the message of prevailing library services in disadvantaged areas appear to carry relatively little impact. The report is critical of much that was observed (for this reason individual programs and cities have not been identified).

As yet, however, the option of self-assessment and appraisal of community needs still remains open to librarians and community leaders. It is a major theme of this book that only through adequate evaluation can the adaptation or shaping of library programs be responsive to social and political needs and successfully meet major service objectives.

THANKS ARE due the many helpful and cooperative urban librarians, particularly the branch librarians, who gave generously of their time to assist in providing requested information.

Valuable counsel and assistance was given by two consultants: Miss Mildred Hennessy, Deputy Director of the Queens Borough Public Library, and Dr. Peter Hiatt, Director of Continuing Education Program for Library Personnel, Western Interstate Commission of Higher Education. Miss Hennessy, in particular, provided many helpful suggestions from her experience in the development of the Langston Hughes Community Library.

Of particular assistance in reviewing the draft report were the following: Dr. Richard Darling, Dean, Columbia University School of Library Service; Dr. Carroll Quigley, History Department, Georgetown University; Mr. Henry Drennan, U. S. Office of Education; and Mr. Clarence Fogelstrom, U. S. Office of Education.

The following Planning Research Corporation staff members contributed substantially to the development and implementation of the study and in the preparation of the final reports: Carolyn Lawall, Ronald Penney, Andrea Smollar. Others participating at various stages of the project included Stephen D. Benson, Ann Carol Brown, William Commins, D. E. Lebby, Susan Levine, Carol Shapiro, Fred Stoffel, and Joyce Taylor.

A special debt of gratitude is owed the Office of Education project officers, Michelle Vale and Arthur Kirschenbaum, for their dedication, interest, and helpfulness. Sincere appreciation is expressed to the numerous other individuals, including community leaders in every city studied, who gave their time for interviews and provided valuable information.

1 Research Method

"IN THE practical sense of doing, research is a matter of techniques. An event occurs or is made to happen by the researcher, and some record of the event occurs or is made. Careful study of the record generates factual statements serviceable as evidence for inferences leading to generalizations, explanations, interpretations, predictions and decisions."[1]

The foregoing quotation summarizes the method generally employed by researchers or evaluators concerned with analysis of programs. This method is the one utilized in this study, in which field visits were made to fifteen cities with library programs serving the economically disadvantaged. In each city a particular branch library located in a low-income area was the focus of study. Data were sought from many sources in order to record, as accurately as possible, the recent progress of the selected branch in providing services to meet the needs of its disadvantaged constituency.

The recording of data for social research purposes is frequently accomplished through one of two common research techniques—the case study and the survey. A case study is a descriptive/analytical study of a particular program, institution, or community, which through its detailed inquiry offers insight into the dynamics of relationships and motivation within the social structure. The drawback to the case study as a research method is that there is no basis for assuming that the insights and experiences of the one

[1] D. B. Gowin and Jason Millman, "Research Methodology—A Point of View," *Review of Educational Research* 39:553 (Dec. 1969).

1

particular unit studied are transferable elsewhere. Survey research, on the other hand, involves the systematic observation of particular variables in a variety of settings and with formal controls such that certain hypotheses can be tested concerning the behavior or other attributes of the studied variables. The drawbacks to survey research on social problems are that it is seldom possible to collect adequate and valid data; it is frequently difficult to quantify and define the variables appropriately; and it is difficult to provide adequate controls in real-life field situations that can preserve the integrity and comparability of the data.

This study represents an effort to pick out major strengths and weaknesses in library programs through the selective use of elements from both the case study and the survey approach. In the style of a case study, we have focused upon a particular geographic area in each city—the neighborhood served by a library branch or special library project—and examined the interaction of residents, library, and other neighborhood institutions in this area in order to illuminate and assess the specific role and potential of the services to the disadvantaged offered. At the same time the study has utilized the survey research approach to the extent feasible, asking the same questions and examining the same variables in each city and using structured interview forms and questionnaires to provide a basis for inference and comparison.

The study design was planned in two phases. First, we planned to look in detail at the individual programs in each city, and second, on the basis of these individual appraisals, we hoped to develop a more detailed and evaluative cross-program analysis of the library programs in relation to the needs and requirements of the groups they are intended to serve (figure 1). To accomplish these purposes, the following research activities were conducted in each city:

1. A detailed examination of library aims and operations
2. An investigation of the library's role in the community as perceived by other community institutions or other library resources with similar or related service goals
3. A survey of community residents, both library users and nonusers, in order to define user needs and requirements.

These data were then assembled and analyzed to generate the findings and recommendations of the study.

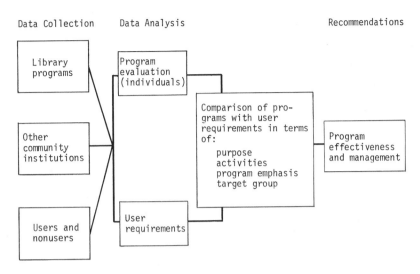

Data Collection   Data Analysis   Recommendations

Figure 1. Data flow

DEFINITION OF TERMS

Certain terms were assigned specific operational definitions. These terms are:

> Library services to the disadvantaged: activity,
>   program, project
> Disadvantaged
> User and potential user; needs and requirements.

Library Services to the Disadvantaged. These are operationally defined in this study to refer to activities or programs undertaken in addition to, or in place of, ordinary library services, with the intention of reaching or serving a disadvantaged population.

A library activity is a physical event or series of repeated events: reading class, art exhibit, open house, story hour, bookmobile visit, assembling of bibliography, and so on.

A library program consists of one or more related activities. A program is identified by the library as an organizational entity ("Tiny Tots Program," "Reader Promotion Program"), has certain specified (though not necessarily formally) objectives, and generally has clearly distinguishable resources assigned to it. The term "project" is used interchangeably with "program" in this study.

Whether or not a particular event is defined in the study as an activity or a program depends largely on how it is structured by the library. A bookmobile operation might constitute a program in one city, while in another city it would be one activity among several in an inner-city program. A story hour in one branch might be regarded as an activity; in another library system story hours might be considered one of the programs. The question of whether a particular event is an activity or a program is important only in assuring common understanding of terms in the study; it has no particular bearing upon data collection outcomes.

Disadvantaged. The focus of the study is upon services to the urban disadvantaged. Operationally, the disadvantaged were defined in the study as individuals residing in low-income neighborhoods. Each of the selected study neighborhoods had previously been classified, usually by the presence of federal programs such as Model Cities, Office of Economic Opportunity projects, or funds from Title I of the Elementary and Secondary Education Act, as a low-income neighborhood.

Libraries serve persons with handicaps other than, or in addition to, those imposed by poverty. Many libraries have services for the blind, the aged, inmates of prisons and hospitals, and so on. However, this study was confined to the economically disadvantaged, i.e., residents of poverty areas.

User and Potential User Requirements. User requirements are defined as implicit or explicit demands for service, interests, or patterns of behavior which users and potential users require to be met or responded to by the library if it wishes to achieve its objectives in relation to them.

It is assumed in the study that the relevant spectrum of user demands would involve library services to be supplied in the following categories: education (formal and informal), information, recreation, and culture. These four service areas constitute the generally accepted dimensions of library services, although not all libraries provide all of these types of service.

A library user was defined as anyone (except staff) encountered in the library, a program participant, or someone not encountered in the library but who had used or visited the library within the last six months. A nonuser, also referred to as a potential user, is anyone who has not been in the library within the last six months. The determination that visiting the library within the last six months be the basis for the classification of users and nonusers is an example of the difficulty involved in quantifying and defining appropriately the relevant variables. How should "users" be defined? Classification could be made according to various criteria, such as recency or frequency of visit, purpose of visit, or possession of a library card. For this study the concept of "library user" was broadly defined to include anyone who is drawn within physical reach of library services and who has entered the library recently enough, i.e., within six months, to have been exposed to whatever service effort is currently being made by the library.

SELECTION OF SAMPLE PROGRAMS

The programs to be studied were selected jointly by the U.S. Office of Education and Planning Research Corporation to incorporate a varied distribution of programs in terms of the following characteristics: nature of the program, size of city, ethnic group served, and geographical location of the city. In addition, the programs were to be currently operating and to have been in operation long enough to generate descriptive and evaluative data.

In each city the selected program was to be studied as it operated through or in relation to the operation of a particular branch library located in a low-income area. In ten of the cities the program was virtually identical with the branch; either the branch was itself a special program or it was a major outlet for the program's activities. In two of these ten cities there was no special program per se, and the branch was studied as a prototype of the city's services to the disadvantaged. In the remaining five cities the selected program was being administered by the central headquarters of the library system and operated through facilities other than those of the branches. In these cities both the program and a branch library serving the disadvantaged were studied, with a view to examining the interaction between the two. In all cases the consent of the appropriate library authority was secured prior to inclusion in the sample.

DATA COLLECTION SOURCES AND INSTRUMENTS

Table 1 lists the data collected in each of the three major data collection instruments: program data, user and nonuser data, and

Table 1. Data Categories

Program Data

Program aims and history (including relation to other library aims and activities)

Program activities (including methods of publicity)

Program resources (materials, equipment, facilities, personnel), costs, and sources of fiscal support

Working relations with other public and private groups or agencies

Current measures of program effectiveness

Program climate: attitudes of project staff, other library staff and library officials involved in the project

Competency and effectiveness of program staff

User/Nonuser Data

Demographic characteristics of users and nonusers

Purposes of users

Attitudes and interests of users and nonusers

Community Data

Socioeconomic characteristics of neighborhood served by branch library or program

Attitudes of public and private community groups working with the disadvantaged toward library facilities, services, and goals

community data. (Major data collection instruments are reproduced in appendix A.)

Data in the *program* category, including initial stimulus for the program, original plans and subsequent modifications, current activities and resources, existing measurements of effectiveness, publicity, involvement of government and other community agencies, and program differences between branch libraries, were collected through interviews with library personnel. Separate structured interview schedules were utilized in interviews with library staff at three levels: the system (chief librarian), the branch (branch librarian), and the program (program director), as well as with a member of the library board of trustees or similar policy-making source. In addition, the operations of the branch or program were observed for several days and informal conversations held with branch staff. Finally, documentary sources, including published and unpublished reports, budgets, and journal and newspaper articles, were consulted.

User and *nonuser* data were collected primarily by means of questionnaires administered orally to library users at the library program/branch location and to users and nonusers in their homes. Library users included a sampling of everyone (eight years of age or older) entering the library. In addition, the questionnaires were administered to a sample of residents living in the neighborhood. If the residents in the sample had *not* visited the library within six months, they were categorized as nonusers. If the residents *had* visited the library within the last six months, they were categorized as "users at home." Data collected from these home users were used as a supplement to other user data.

Community data were collected from several sources. In each city structured interviews were held with:

1. The director of the poverty center or agency operating in the selected branch neighborhood
2. The school librarian and the principal or an assistant principal of both a public and a private (serving neighborhood students) school in the selected branch neighborhood, at a level (i.e., elementary or secondary) appropriate to the program being studied
3. A representative of the city government at the highest policy level at which general familiarity with library programs also exists.

These interviews were intended to elicit the respondents' perceptions of community needs, their knowledge of library programs and project purposes, and their view of the library's role as a community institution.

The views held by these individuals represent, it is assumed, a distillation of the experience of the community with respect to the library branch, based on some years of exposure to its activities, its staff, its "image." The representatives of these agencies, it is further assumed, would be more likely than the average resident to be aware of the library's role in the context of community needs and existing services within the broad educational spectrum. These data thus provide a basis for assessment of library program impact generally in the community, supplementing the data collected from other sources.

DATA COLLECTION METHODS

Two study teams were formed, with each team having one senior interviewer and one or two junior interviewers. Each team visited half the sample programs. Field visits in each city lasted approximately five working days, during which period all interviewing of library staff, community agencies, and users and nonusers of the library took place.

Pretest visits to the first two cities were scheduled in August 1969; return visits to regather user data in these cities were made during January and February 1970. Visits to the remaining thirteen cities were made during the fall and winter months and completed in February 1970.

In each city the senior interviewer conducted the interviews with library staff and other organizational representatives, and the other team members supervised the collection of user/nonuser questionnaire data. These data were collected in each city by teams of neighborhood residents, recruited and trained by Planning Research Corporation staff. The utilization of neighborhood residents as interviewers was designed to provide a comfortable interpersonal contact between interviewer and subject, and to elicit a genuine response, as free as possible of a social desirability "set." In Spanish-speaking areas bilingual interviewers were employed and furnished with Spanish translations of the user/nonuser questionnaires. In each city 80 users and 120 nonusers were interviewed by these local teams.

User data were collected primarily from individuals entering the library. Children under the age of eight were not interviewed; children between the ages of eight and twelve were administered a shortened form of the interview questionnaire; they were asked questions appropriate for their age group.

It was noted in pretests that the majority of users were school-age children, and that these children tended to arrive in pairs or groups of two or more and to peak during the after-school hours. One or two interviewers, therefore, were stationed in the library and instructed to collect interviews from all persons using the library;

during peak hours when it might not be possible to interview every-one, they were instructed to collect interviews from at least one of each pair or group of users arriving together. (There were vir-tually no refusals or nonrespondents.)

A total of 1,177 library users were interviewed in the branch libraries or program locations. In some cities it was not possible to collect the required number of 80 user interviews in the library or program location, chiefly because the number of weekly users was small (many users come frequently during the week, but these were not knowingly interviewed more than once). In these cases the required number was achieved by including some interviews with users at home; 159 of these interviews were used.

Nonuser data were obtained from 1,778 library nonusers by visiting the homes of a sample of neighborhood residents living within a half-mile radius of the selected branch library. All of the subjects were thirteen or more years of age; there were no other requirements for inclusion in the sample beyond the stratification in each neighborhood designed to sample more heavily in blocks closest to the library. A resident was classified as a nonuser if he stated that he had not visited the library within the preceding six months. (If he had visited the library during this period, he was classified as a user at home.)

A more detailed description of the user/nonuser data collection methods and analytical procedures is presented in appendix B.

DATA ANALYSIS

The user/nonuser data were computer-tabulated, and responses to each item were cross-tabulated by user and nonuser categories and by city. A separate analysis was subsequently made of the user-at-home data, using all of the 569 questionnaires in this group and comparing them with those obtained from nonusers.

The program and community data that were collected were assembled initially in the form of individual profiles or narratives describing and analyzing the programs in each city. These indi-vidual program profiles attempted to answer the questions of whether or not the programs were successful in meeting their own objectives and responsive to the needs and interests of the con-stituency. The programs were appraised in terms of a basic systems analysis approach, which is described in chapter 4. This conceptual framework focuses upon those aspects of program strategy, including objectives, planning, and implementation, that are general, replicable, and within the control of the program developer or administrator. Major findings were presented in two reports to the U.S. Office of Education. The material contained in these reports has been revised for presentation in the following chapters.

Chapters 2 and 3 set out to define the concept of "user requirements" in terms of the population to be served and the environmental context in which service is delivered. Chapter 2 describes the target groups in the low-income urban neighborhoods that were visited and reports the results of the user/nonuser survey in regard to relevant characteristics of individuals, indicators of their needs and interests, and their views on library-related matters. Chapter 3 then summarizes the information from the fifteen cities concerning the community context of library services and presents a view of the library in relation to similar services and resources already available to these same groups in the community. The community context also includes a generalized assessment of community needs in the broad educational spectrum and of library capacity to meet these needs, as expressed by representatives of community agencies.

Chapters 4 and 5 provide an analytical framework for planning and evaluating library services to the disadvantaged, relating them to the concepts of client need and social utility developed in the preceding two chapters. The analytical approach elaborates, from the data collected during the visits to the fifteen library programs, concepts of program effectiveness and program impact and examines related measurement issues.

Chapters 6 through 11 present selected portions of the individual city profiles from which chapters 2–5 were developed. These selections are intended to highlight points made in the general analysis, illustrating the way in which various program strategies result in the successes or the frustrations of day-to-day program operations. Chapter 12 provides a summary and conclusions.

2 Problems of Library Service to the Disadvantaged

HOW CAN the public library best serve the urban disadvantaged? In forming a research hypothesis to address this question, it was clear that the purposes or goals of the library in relation to this group must be defined. A review of what has been written on this subject revealed a variety of approaches and some conflict and confusion among librarians as to what the goals of library service to the disadvantaged should be.

THE LIBRARY AS A SOCIAL INSTITUTION

According to one traditional view, the major function of libraries as social institutions is the collection, organization, and dissemination of knowledge and information through printed and other materials. In pursuing this function, the library is likely to view itself as a resource, a repository of information, and to be concerned primarily with the flow of that information, with materials rather than people. The library meets the needs of users by making available and accessible appropriate materials, but it does not assume responsibility for attracting users or for inducing changes in the pattern or scope of use.

A somewhat broader view of the library's goals sees the library as active, concerned with interpersonal relationships, involved, an agent in social and individual change. Proponents of this role argue that the library has no alternative but to adopt this position. The disadvantaged do not use the library; the reasons why they do not use it include illiteracy, ignorance, apathy, and hostility. To ~overcome these powerful obstacles, the library must actively, energetically, and physically seek out and involve the groups they wish to reach. The responsibility of the library is extended from that of supplying information to that of actively seeking to modify individual behavior and attitudes.[1]

The unanswered and difficult questions about library services seem to focus in this area. Can libraries persuade disadvantaged persons to use their facilities by concentrating primarily on attractive and relevant materials and on accessibility? Is active outreach and involvement also necessary? Is it necessary for all groups? Where it is necessary, how extensive should it be? How successful is it likely to be? How costly will it be?

The modifications or expansion of the library role that would be necessary to stimulate social change are regarded in some quarters as innovative, if not avant-garde. However, there is ample historical precedent for this function of actively promoting individual change. The public library system had its origins in the last century, along with numerous related movements concerned with individual growth and development—mental health, child development, counseling, and guidance. According to one account, the purpose of these first libraries was "to give the common man facilities for self-education so that he could use his vote wisely."[2] In another account the purpose was "to facilitate the assimilation of European immigrants to the urban, middle-class, American style of life."[3] In either case, helping, educating, and changing people was the goal.

The rationale for the existence of the public library as a social institution rests upon a premise of social utility. The hallmark of library success or effectiveness must therefore inevitably be the number of users from the target population. Other measures of effectiveness may be devised to guide the components of program planning and allocation of resources, but this is an essential criterion.

---

[1] For a discussion of how the function of supplying and interpreting information can, and should, involve inner-city libraries in an active, advocacy role for social justice and reform, see Mary Lee Bundy, "Urban Information and Public Libraries: A Design for Service," *Library Journal* 97:161–69 (Jan. 15, 1972).

[2] George Chandler, *Libraries in the Modern World* (Oxford: Pergamon Press, 1965), p.22.

[3] Edward C. Banfield, "Needed: A Public Purpose," in *The Public Library and the City*, R. W. Conant, ed. (Cambridge, Mass.: MIT Press, 1965), p. 104–5.

As Gans has pointed out, a library must of necessity be user-oriented because "if a library is not attractive to many users, it is difficult to demand for it a large share of scarce public resources. A library that is not used sufficiently is a waste of resources, even if its goals are noble and the size and quality of the collection are outstanding."[4]

The argument is made that institutions or agencies of artistic and literary excellence, preserving and communicating man's humanistic heritage, should be supported and maintained by government subsidy if necessary, even if they do not command broad popular support or conform to popular tastes. In the United States public support of such institutions has been somewhat arbitrary; many libraries and museums, and more recently some educational television, have been supported by tax revenues, whereas most symphony orchestras and drama, opera, and dance companies have not. There has been no consistent rationale for continued public support or nonsupport for any one of these. There is, therefore, no reason to assume that public support of public libraries at the local level will be sustained indefinitely at the more or less constant rate that has been maintained for the past 20–25 years. In fact, in recent years the proportion of city expenditures going to libraries in the larger cities has begun to show a slight but noticeable decline.[5] In all cities, large and small, financial and social responsibilities of local governments have increased substantially, while available revenues have diminished. The growing urban fiscal crisis requires even more stringent priorities in allocation of resources, particularly in meeting the needs of the disadvantaged. Therefore greater accountability will surely be required of libraries, as of other community services, and their services evaluated in a more rigorous way.

These considerations have served to generate the major hypothesis for the present study. This hypothesis may be stated as follows: To be effective, library services to the disadvantaged should meet the needs and requirements of users and potential users. Public libraries must be able to define the unmet needs of their disadvantaged constituencies, to analyze the problems underlying those needs, and to derive from this analysis appropriate goals and objectives.

[4] Herbert J. Gans, "The Public Library in Perspective," in R. W. Conant, ed., *Public Library and the City*, p.69.
[5] Tom Childers and Beth Krevitt, "Municipal Funding of Library Services," *American Libraries* 3:56 (Jan. 1972).

To gain insight into the needs and requirements of these library users and potential users, more than 3,000 individuals in fifteen cities, residents of low-income urban areas living within half a mile of a branch library, were interviewed as a part of this study (appendix table 1).

CHARACTERISTICS OF USERS AND NONUSERS

The survey provides some interesting and useful information concerning library users and nonusers. For example, two-thirds of the library users in ghetto areas identified in this study were under the age of nineteen; one-third were of elementary school age (twelve and under). The younger children come to the library more often than the older ones; 70 percent of the twelve-and-under group come at least once a week. In general, those that do patronize the library come often; more than half come at least once a week, and roughly another 25 percent come at least once a month. The 50–65 percent of library users who come frequently have probably also been users over a period of some duration. About 60 percent of users have been coming to the library for more than two years, and more than half used another library before coming to their present one. Two-thirds of the users have cards; the rest do not.

The most frequently given reason for coming to the library is related to school work. The next most frequent reasons for coming are to read in the library, to take out novels for enjoyment, and to be with friends. Three of these four reasons, i.e., all except taking novels, are associated primarily with youthful patronage.

Most of the young children (80 percent) live within six blocks of the library, and almost all of them (90 percent) walk. Adult users tend to live somewhat further away and either walk (55–60 percent) or come in a car (30 percent). Hardly anyone uses public transportation to reach the library.

The data suggest that the self-selection process by which individuals beyond elementary school age become or fail to become library users is related to the socioeconomic variables of income and education. For example, only 20 percent of library users in low-income areas report family incomes of less than $100 per week,[6] whereas 40 percent of nonusers in the same neighborhoods report incomes this low. Ten percent of library users thirteen years of

[6] Users thirteen years of age and over. See notes to appendix table 1.

age and over have finished college, as compared to 2 percent of nonusers, and 60 percent of library users thirteen years and over are in school.[7]

Library users of all ages are more knowledgeable concerning cultural events, community institutions, and community resources. Approximately half of all the low-income library users have been to a museum, concert, or art exhibit, as compared to 20–30 percent of nonusers. Among users over the age of twelve, about 60 percent have heard of the local poverty agencies, preschool programs, basic education programs, and employment centers intended to serve the disadvantaged in their neighborhood. On the average, about 20 percent of these have used these services. Among nonusers about 45 percent have heard of these agencies, but only 15 percent have used them, despite the higher incidence of poverty in this group.

Twenty-five percent of nonusers have never heard of their branch or neighborhood library. Of those who have heard of it, only one-third remember having ever visited it. Almost all the nonusers who have heard of the library know that it has books, but they are not well informed about other materials or activities. Users are obviously more knowledgeable about library materials, and half of them know something about the library's special programs or activities.

Despite these significant differences between library users and library nonusers, there are fundamental preferences common to both, particularly in the area of media and communication. For example, 90 percent of all the persons interviewed—children and adults—watch television, and 60 percent watch it every day. More than 80 percent of those over twelve usually read the papers, and roughly the same proportion listen to the radio. However, despite the fact that virtually everyone is reached by these media, the most common way in which young adult and adult users and nonusers find out about community programs or services is through friends, neighbors, or other members of the family. Only about 10–15 percent find out about these programs through radio, television, or newspapers. Perhaps it may be more accurate to say that individuals do not fully internalize what the community programs offer or consist of until they hear about the programs directly from another person.

[7] For the U.S. population at large, about 30 percent were in school in 1966. (U.S. Dept. of Commerce, *Statistical Abstract of the United States, 1969* [Washington: Govt. Printing Office, 1969], p.101, 111.)

Users and nonusers thirteen years of age and over were asked to select from a list of library materials and activities those that would be of interest to them. The choices made most frequently by both groups were print materials—books, magazines, and newspapers. Users expressed an interest almost equally strong in information on job training and other community services. The next most popular choice was free entertainment, such as movies, dances, and music. Nonusers were generally less interested in any of the items on the list, but about half expressed interest in children's programs and in adult education.

The same users and nonusers were asked to choose subjects of interest from a list that included child care, medical information, legal help, job information, and similar areas related to daily life. Responses to these items are apparently reflections of the sex and age differences between users and nonusers, rather than of differences related to socioeconomic variables. The most frequent choices of users are sports, job information, and racial discrimination. The most frequent choices of nonusers are medical information or help, child care, and job information. The interest in employment and related information is pervasive; higher percentages of users and nonusers had used or visited employment centers than other community programs.

Of all persons interviewed, approximately 60 percent were black, 10 percent Spanish-speaking, and the remaining 30 percent white. These proportions are the same for both library users and nonusers. The interviews were conducted in eight city neighborhoods that were predominantly black, two neighborhoods that were predominantly white, two that were mixed or contiguous black and white neighborhoods, and three that were predominantly Spanish-speaking.

The principal difference among these communities that emerges from the data is the relative absence of adult users in black neighborhoods (table 2). At least, the absence of adult users is more conspicuous in the libraries serving black neighborhoods; it may be characteristic to a lesser degree of all libraries located in low-income areas. These low-income libraries retain the youth/student component of library patronage, a component which also accounts for about half of standard library users, but are lacking in varying degrees in patronage by nonstudent users.

These central findings that library use is related to income and education and that library users tend to be predominantly school-

Table 2. Percentage of Adult Users (Age 19 and Over)

Black Neighborhoods	Percentage of Adult Library Users
1	5
2	*
3	14
4	5
5	8
6	10
7	11
8	34**
Mixed Neighborhoods	
1	45
2	31
White Neighborhoods	
1	22
2	44
Spanish-Speaking Neighborhoods	
1	27
2	52
3	32

* No figure shown because 50 percent of users interviewed in this city were students in adult education classes using library materials and were not individuals found in the library.
** This library was located in an adult service facility, which doubtless accounts for the unusually high percent of adult users.

age children and young adults, with relatively few adult users, requires further analysis for several reasons. First, it is inadequate and simplistic to ascribe library use directly to socioeconomic level without a more detailed examination of the variables. Second, the user/nonuser comparisons that have been described above would be quite useless for library planning if these differences are due primarily to the fact that, statistically speaking, these are two different populations, i.e., children and adults, respectively, rather than samples of users and nonusers drawn from a single population. Finally, we would like to know more about why so few adults in hard-core black poverty areas utilize the library's resources, and in what ways libraries might be able to provide more effective services to them.

Therefore, a separate tabulation and analysis was made of a subgroup of users and nonusers (excluding children under thirteen) identified as drawn from a single statistical population but differentiated in terms of library use or nonuse. This subset includes all library users and nonusers located *at home* during the household phase of the neighborhood surveys, and is further classified according to racial or ethnic origin.[8] Table 3 presents the characteristics of this subgroup of users and nonusers in terms of the arithmetic mean of their responses to selected questions from the survey questionnaire. This table is essentially a condensed version of the kind of information shown in appendix table 2; in table 3 the distribution of user and nonuser responses to each question has been compressed to the means, which are shown as coded for computer analysis. Using the interpretation of the code also given in table 3 permits us to describe this subgroup as the total group has been described above, i.e., in terms of general comparisons between users and nonusers.

The principal differences between users and nonusers that were noted in the data describing the total group in appendix table 1 are sustained in this subgroup. Thus we see that, even after excluding the youngest category from the sample and considering only those older than twelve, users remain a somewhat younger group than nonusers. Perhaps this effect is entirely due to the heavy library use by those aged thirteen to eighteen, since some of them are included in this sample. From variable 2 we see that three-fourths of those interviewed were women, but there does not seem to be much difference in library use by sex. Because the sampling technique was biased against the selection of working men, we might make a very vague guess that women are more frequent users than men, but that remains only a guess. Variable 3 was present for coding reasons in this study.

We see that users are somewhat more educated and that the percentage of users currently enrolled in an educational program is between two and a half to four times higher than that of nonusers, depending upon race. On the next variable, family size, we see that users have slightly larger families, but this may be explained by a sampling effect. Any reader in the 13–18-year-old category is necessarily a member of a family with children. Not too much difference shows up in employment status; however, we see that there is a considerable income difference, indicating that there is probably an actual employment difference also.

[8] For further details of this tabulation and analysis see appendix B.

Table 3.   Coded Group Mean Scores on All Variables, by Library Use or Nonuse and by Ethnic Groups

Variables	Range	Interpretation of Code / Directional Significance: The Higher—	Users			Nonusers			Combined Users & Nonusers		
			White	Black	Spanish Surname	White	Black	Spanish Surname	White	Black	Spanish Surname
1. Age	1-9	The older	7.07	6.52	6.75	7.49	7.12	7.13	7.37	7.02	6.96
2. Sex	1-2	More female	1.77	1.75	1.81	1.79	1.79	1.82	1.78	1.78	1.81
3. Race *	1-3	More white	3.00	1.00	—	3.00	1.00	—	3.00	1.00	—
4. Educational level	1-8	More educated	4.88	4.42	3.70	4.19	3.87	3.42	4.39	3.97	3.54
5. Currently in educational program	1-2	Less in school	1.82	1.75	1.79	1.95	1.94	1.92	1.92	1.91	1.87
6. Family size	1-4	Larger	1.70	2.05	2.10	1.54	1.83	1.98	1.59	1.87	2.03
7. Employment status	1-2	Less employed	1.55	1.49	1.66	1.58	1.54	1.66	1.57	1.54	1.66
8. Income	1-5	Higher	3.11	3.23	2.86	2.67	2.57	2.56	2.79	2.69	2.69
9. Daily life subjects of interest	0-10	More interests	3.42	3.90	3.96	2.81	3.17	3.20	2.98	3.30	3.53
10. Interest in library materials	0-4	More interests	2.45	2.16	2.44	1.79	1.57	1.87	1.92	1.68	2.12
11. Interest in library services	0-5	More interests	2.58	2.69	2.85	2.00	2.22	2.13	2.16	2.30	2.44
12. Image of library	0-5	More positive	4.07	3.42	3.77	3.26	2.89	3.18	3.49	2.99	3.44
13. Knowledge of local poverty agency	0-2	More knowledge	.76	.97	.80	.53	.68	.68	.59	.73	.73
14. Knowledge of local preschool	0-2	More knowledge	.83	1.06	.90	.66	.86	.83	.72	.90	.86
15. Knowledge of local adult education	0-2	More knowledge	.87	.91	.79	.60	.71	.56	.68	.74	.66
16. Knowledge of local job information	0-2	More knowledge	.79	1.13	.98	.62	.87	.92	.67	.92	.95
17. Knowledge of various community resources	0-10	More knowledge	6.67	4.87	4.66	4.53	3.27	4.09	5.14	3.55	4.34
18. Read newspapers last week	0-1	More reading	.62	.58	.51	.62	.52	.48	.62	.53	.49
19. Read magazines last week	0-1	More reading	.53	.36	.34	.38	.22	.26	.42	.25	.29
20. Read books last week	0-1	More reading	.51	.48	.40	.28	.26	.21	.34	.30	.29
21. Read something last week	1-2	Less reading	1.09	1.10	1.19	1.22	1.25	1.30	1.18	1.23	1.26
22. Watched TV last week	1-2	Less viewing	1.07	1.07	1.07	1.09	1.13	1.07	1.09	1.12	1.07
23. Listened to radio last week	1-2	Less listening	1.17	1.18	1.20	1.24	1.20	1.20	1.22	1.20	1.20
24. Attended cultural events: museum, concert, art exhibit, during last yr.	0-3	Wider attendance	1.46	1.28	1.16	.73	.66	.72	.94	.77	.91

*Mean score for combined black/white groups: users 2.08, nonusers 1.77.

We see that users score higher on our next three variables, which have to do with measuring the subject's interests. The next variable, image of the library, indicates that between races, the black group has a much lower image of the library than the white and the Spanish-surname groups. This may have considerable consequences. We see, however, that library users have a very much higher image of the library than nonusers, so as a consequence black users have a better image of the library than white nonusers.

The next five variables measure knowledge of community resources, and we see that the users score somewhat higher on all of these. On the next four reading variables, we see little difference in newspaper reading. The users do significantly more magazine, book, and overall reading. Roughly one-half of library users had read a book during the previous week, as compared to one-fourth of nonusers. Almost everyone watches television and listens to the radio, and the differences between users and nonusers are not pronounced. The last variable, attendance at cultural events, shows the users far out in front. There are some racial differences present, but the user-nonuser difference is the dominating one.

Having established these differences between users and nonusers, we are interested in some effort to sort out the various effects that have been observed in the hope of discerning some of the dynamics of library use. A method of statistical analysis has therefore been applied which is intended to accomplish this. The method is discriminant analysis, which as applied to the surveyed library users and nonusers allows an optimal assignment of an unsurveyed person to one of two groups on the basis of his attributes, exclusive of library use.

The analysis provides a statistical method for estimating the relative contribution to library use of each factor or attribute. This estimate is adjusted to take into consideration the effect of the other variables. It attempts to provide answers such as would reliably have been obtained by the classic experimental method. Suppose, for example, that library usage were known to depend on just two variables, school status and attendance at cultural events such as museums, concerts, and art exhibits. If the two independent variables were perfectly correlated, i.e., if only school children attended cultural events, then the effect on library use of attendance at cultural events for those not in school would not be determinable. At the other extreme, the effect of each variable could be precisely estimated if an experiment could be devised that would assign people randomly to four neighborhoods, each having a library but one having no access either to school or to museums, etc.; one having access to school but not to museums, etc.; one with access to museums, etc., but not school; and the fourth with access to both.

Usually none of these extremes prevails, and the effect of each of the partly correlated variables must be assessed on the basis of a statistical model, such as that furnished by discriminant analysis. Discriminant analysis is most reliable when the variables being examined are relatively independent of one another. Since most of the correlations among variables in the analysis are in the neutral range,[9] this does not appear to be a serious drawback in the present instance.

Discriminant analysis produces a set of coefficients, one for each variable, which in effect sort the individual into either the user or nonuser group. A more readily scalable measurement of effect, also generated by the discriminant analysis, is the *F* ratio associated with each of the variables.

This *F* ratio for a given variable is a measure of how much a particular variable contributes to the overall analysis. It is obtained by constructing a discriminant function from the remaining variables with that particular variable deleted, and its reduced discriminating power is then compared to the discriminating function which had included all the variables. The *F* ratio is high when the second function does much more poorly than the first, telling us that the particular variable was apparently quite important.

The results of the discriminant analysis are shown in table 4, and the balance of this chapter discusses these findings. Some caution is urged in attempting to interpret these results. For one thing, the extent to which true differences between users and nonusers can be explained by the data is limited. The proportion of variance between users and nonusers that is explained by the entered variables in the analysis is as follows:

Whites	.23
Blacks	.19
Spanish-surname	.20
Combined blacks and whites	.20

[9] Correlation matrices were constructed for all variables.

Table 4. Critical F Ratios for Variables at Significance Levels, upon Entry and at Conclusion of Discriminant Analysis, by Racial or Ethnic Group

Variables	Whites F values to enter	Whites Final F values	Blacks F values to enter	Blacks Final F values	Spanish Surname F values to enter	Spanish Surname Final F values	Combined Blacks & Whites F values to enter	Combined Blacks & Whites Final F values
1. Age	4.74	7.84						
2. Sex								
3. Race								
4. Education level	4.97	4.64					13.76	15.70
5. Currently in education program	-17.14	-24.66	-97.55	-48.09	-6.78		6.93	5.21
6. Family size							-71.40	-68.07
7. Employment status								
8. Income			32.06	15.58			19.55	17.64
9. Daily life subjects of interest			3.99					
10. Interest in library materials								
11. Interest in library services					11.30			
12. Image of library	17.11	8.62			10.35			
13. Knowledge of local poverty agency	10.84	9.17	-21.42	6.52		10.56	32.31	9.30
14. Knowledge of preschool			6.06				19.24	18.52
15. Knowledge of local adult education	8.58	4.20			5.19	8.38	5.82	6.36
16. Knowledge of local job information								
17. Knowledge of various community resources	97.15	23.17	14.16				91.55	29.23
18. Read newspapers last week		-8.44					-7.53	-7.53
19. Read magazines last week								
20. Read books last week							12.99	4.84
21. Read something last week	-3.85		-8.53				-4.22	-10.17
22. Watched TV last week								
23. Listened to radio last week								
24. Attended cultural events: museum, concert, art exhibit, during last yr.	53.88	14.45	51.50	11.91	13.04		185.56	27.66

Critical F values: $F_{.05} = 3.84$; $F_{.01} = 6.63$; $F_{.005} = 7.87$; $F_{.001} = 10.8$.

The signs prefixed to the Final F ratios have been taken from the discriminant function coefficients. Their directional meaning is shown in table 3. In general, positive signs indicate a larger contribution to or explanation of use. However, this meaning is reversed for variables 5 and 21.

The explained variance thus runs at about 20 percent, within the usual range of research findings relating socioeconomic variables to broadly educational outcomes. For example, Wilson comments that "sets of socioeconomic indices rarely account for more than 30 percent of the variance in IQ test scores. A more extensive set, including race and neighborhood status, accounted for only 15 percent of the variance in primary grade IQ test scores in [a particular study]."[10]

Since a substantial portion of the variance is not explained, there is reason to consider that the analysis may not be reaching or identifying major motivators to library use or nonuse. On the other hand, the factors that do emerge as significant can reasonably be assessed as likely hypotheses upon which to base library policies and planning.

Within this caveat, the analysis points up subtle but important differences between the subsets of adult users and adult nonusers that were not apparent when all users (including children) were compared with all nonusers.

First, the most powerful variable generally distinguishing adult users from nonusers is found to be current enrollment in some sort of educational or vocational program (variable 5). For adults as well as children participation in some formal educational program, either in or out of the school system, is apparently the single most powerful motivator for library use. The next most powerful variables are those associated with attendance at popular or classical cultural events. The implication here seems to be the presence of the same general motivation which also causes people to use the library. Some measure of familiarity with community resources is also important. If we consider variables 13, 14, 15, 16, and 17 as a group (dealing with community facilities), we find that at least one is included as a differentiating variable for each ethnic group, and we may interpret these as representing a fairly high level of environmental competence. Thus, the individuals who patronize the library are apparently more interested in upward mobility for themselves, more responsive to presentations of ideas and feelings in nonprint media, and more knowledgeable concerning their community and its affairs.

Further, the analysis indicates differences between racial and

[10] Alan B. Wilson, "Social Class and Equal Educational Opportunity," *Harvard Educational Review* 31:83 (1968).

ethnic groups which, if generally true, would have important implications for differential programming. In general, the identifiable factors that contribute significantly to library use are varied and cover a fairly wide range of implied purpose and motivation; however, there appear to be clearly defined differences in pattern among the three major groups studied. The following paragraphs present major findings for each of the three groups: whites, blacks, and Spanish-surnamed.

Whites. Several variables were shown to contribute significantly to differences between white users and white nonusers:

Variable	F Ratio
5. Currently in educational program	24.66
17. Knowledge of various community resources	23.17
24. Attendance at cultural events	14.45
13. Knowledge of local poverty agency	9.17
12. Image of library	8.62
18. Newspaper reading	−8.45
1. Age	7.84
4. Educational level	4.64
15. Knowledge of local adult education program	4.20

The first variable is educational enrollment; the largest F ratio, and therefore the most powerful variable in differentiating between users and nonusers, is found to be current enrollment in some sort of educational or vocational program. The next most powerful variables are those associated with knowledge of community resources and attendance at cultural events. Variable 17 measures the subject's awareness of where in his community he could get information on a list of specific subjects related to daily life: child care, medical help, legal help, sports, and so on. The next variable (24), attendance at a museum, concert, or art exhibit, was defined to include rock or jazz concerts and amateur, pop, or African art exhibits, i.e., "popular" culture as well as the classical variety. Variable 13, knowledge of the local community action or poverty agency, is similar to variable 17 in its implications.

It is interesting to note that none of these three variables—17, 24, or 13—necessarily involves extensive use of print materials. It is interesting further to note that these variables outweigh those traditionally thought to be of major importance, i.e., income and level of educational achievement. (Level of educational achievement, variable 4, refers to school grade completed: grammar school, high school, college, etc. This variable is not the same as variable 5, which registers current participation in an educational program at any level.) Although there are modest correlations between variable 8 (income) and variables 17 and 24, and between variable 4 (education) and variables 17 and 24, the more personally oriented characteristics are more important in describing the library user. In the presence of these variables of knowledge of community resources and attendance at cultural events, income is reduced to less than statistical significance, and education appears just above the critical level.

Image of the library (variable 12) also distinguishes between white users and nonusers. It is not at all clear whether image is formed as a result of library use or independently. Some older black subjects in the South, for example, stated that they could remember when public libraries were segregated, and this obviously created for them an image based on nonuse. In any event, white users are much more likely than nonusers to perceive the library as a friendly, busy place in which an average adult, not just a student or a serious reader, can feel comfortable.

Newspaper reading (variable 18) is of special interest here because of relationships with variables 19, 20, and 21. The original questionnaire item asked first: "Did you read something last week?" (variable 21). The subject could then respond by indicating that he read books (variable 20), magazines (variable 19), newspapers (variable 18), or any combination of these. Interpretation of the negative value for newspaper reading therefore seems to be that, when the contribution of books and magazines is entered into account, the net marginal contribution of reading the newspaper is associated with *not* using the library. In effect, people who read only newspapers tend not to use the library, and people who read newspapers and also other materials tend to be library users.

Age (variable 1) shows up as a distinguishing variable between white users and white nonusers, with users being significantly older than nonusers. This finding, counter to the general direction for this variable, seems to be a residual effect. All of the whites interviewed were, on the average, older than the minority group users and nonusers (see group means, table 3). This may reflect a residency pattern in low-income areas in which numbers of elderly poor whites (the mean age category for this group is 40–60 years) both reside in white communities and linger on in nonwhite communities.

After the library users in educational programs have been accounted for, a significant portion of the remaining library users may perhaps be drawn from this category of older residents.

The last two variables that differentiate between users and nonusers are level of educational achievement and knowledge of community adult education programs. It is interesting to find these two together, since the educational achievement variable is traditionally associated, in the context of library usage, with formal education beyond high school, whereas adult education programs in low-income areas are generally oriented toward basic education.

This finding reinforces the notion that library use is not associated directly with socioeconomic level, i.e., with the leisure or the more sophisticated intellectual interests or the greater involvement in literary issues that might characterize middle-class users. Rather it is associated with participation in a formal educational program, which can involve individuals at either end of the economic spectrum.

Blacks. In some ways the pattern of library use by blacks resembles that of whites. Several of the same factors contribute significantly to differences between black users and black nonusers:

Variable	F Ratio
5. Currently in educational program	48.09
8. Income	15.58
24. Attendance at cultural events	11.91
13. Knowledge of local poverty agency	6.52

Three of the discriminating variables—participation in an educational program, attendance at cultural events, and knowledge of the local poverty program—are the same for whites and nonwhites. The student and the active citizen predominate as library users.

There is an important departure from the pattern associated with whites, however, in that income appears as a discriminating variable. The implications of this are by no means definitive: Income has emerged as a variable discriminating between black users and nonusers chiefly because less is explained by the analysis about its relation to other variables. For example, it may be that the lowest-income blacks in urban areas are those most recently migrated from Southern states, with a negative view of the library as a result of being refused access in the past. Or it may be that differences in income emerge because the poorest individuals, absorbed in the struggle for survival, do not find library services relevant or useful. As a group (users and nonusers together) blacks are poorer than the white or the Spanish-surnamed group, yet black users emerge as more affluent than other users. In effect, individuals with higher income levels are over-represented among black users.

If this interpretation of the inhibiting effects of lowest-income levels upon library use is in fact valid, then it places severe limitations upon what library programs for the disadvantaged can hope to accomplish. Libraries can hope to change their image or to expand their student clientele, but there is little they can do to change or otherwise overcome the level of financial poverty and its apparent implications, particularly in hard-core areas.

Spanish-Surnamed. The Spanish-surnamed group of users and nonusers is much smaller than the other groups, which accounts in part for the fact that only two variables have values above the significance level when all variables are entered into the analysis:

Variable	F Ratio
12. Image of library	10.56
15. Knowledge of local adult education program	8.38

In view of the relatively small size of the sample, we may wish to look at the next two variables which showed up as significant during the stepwise procedure but whose final values were depressed below the significance level:

11. Interest in library services
17. Knowledge of various community resources

With these four variables we have a dominant pattern associated with reaction to the library and with adult education that is different from that shown by the other ethnic groups.

The predominance of the library image variable as a net contributor to library use over and above all other variables suggests two possible interpretations. First, Spanish-surnamed people may in fact be strongly influenced for or against library use by the image of their particular neighborhood branch. It should be noted that Mexican-Americans, at any rate, are unlikely to have *preconceived* ideas about public libraries, since there are none in Mexico.

A second interpretation of the predominance of the library image variable is that it arises as a result of the presence of a language barrier. Other variables that distinguish the white and black library user fail to appear here, perhaps because such activities are limited, for both user and nonuser, by language barriers and/or by social or cultural isolation. Variable 15, reflecting knowledge of local adult education programs, which in Spanish-speaking communities mainly consist of English classes, tends to reinforce the interpretation of the language barrier as keeping many Spanish-surnamed Americans away from the libraries and effectively "washing away" differences between individuals or groups that might otherwise emerge.

Comparison of Black/White Users and Nonusers. The above analyses have made no attempt to assess the impact of race as a variable when entered with the other variables. The meaning of race, if entered as a factor, is very unclear in the context of this study; to say that whites patronize a library more or less frequently than blacks is essentially to affirm merely that there are motivations or explanations for this behavior not identified by the variables defined in the study. However, since the blacks and whites in the study have several common characteristics that contribute significantly to library usage, it was thought to be of some interest to enter the elements that are encompassed in the factor of race, in order to see whether this factor would result in any changes in the order of the others. This analysis does not include the Spanish-surnamed group.

Variable	F Ratio
5. Currently in educational program	68.07
17. Knowledge of various community resources	29.23
24. Attendance at cultural events	27.66
13. Knowledge of local poverty agency	18.52
8. Income	17.64
3. Race	15.70
21. General reading	10.17
12. Image of library	9.30
18. Newspaper reading	7.53
14. Knowledge of preschool programs	6.36
4. Educational level	5.21
20. Book reading	4.84

The results, as shown above, demonstrate the primacy of the same variables that appeared as most powerful in the two groups when analyzed separately, i.e., current enrollment in an educational program, knowledge of community resources, and attendance at cultural events. These factors outweigh all of the others, including income, race, and educational level, in their net contribution to library usage.

The entry of race as a variable is also related to the appearance of three new variables, two of them related to reading and one to knowledge of preschool programs. For variables 14 and 20, at the bottom of the list, i.e., just above the cutoff level for statistical significance, it is possible that increased sample size and small realignments in all of the factors resulted in their moving up over the cutoff level. The appearance of variable 21 in the middle of the list, however, may be interpreted to mean that reading becomes a discriminating factor when the variable of race is entered. We should interpret this as follows: Within each group the users read more than nonusers, but as other variables are entered in the analysis, they apparently are able to explain the reading variable to the extent that after these variables are present, the reading variable tells us nothing further about library use. When we combine the two groups, we are in some sense averaging over the two discriminant functions, which would not be as good as the original functions for discriminating within either of the two groups. Thus we might not have explained the reading variable as well as before by means of the other variables, so the reading variable still can tell us something about library use and consequently has shown up in the list.

SUMMARY

There are several implications of the findings detailed in this chapter. The data suggest several problem areas to which library program and policy planning should be addressed. First, the program and materials orientation of most libraries is of interest to low-income subjects primarily while they are involved in some type of formal educational program. The principal characteristic distinguishing users from nonusers is participation in school or in some other type of educational program (e.g., adult education, or an educational component of a vocational program). Since the total number of adults in educational programs is likely to be a relatively small proportion of the population, the potential adult target group for library services on this basis is quite limited. (Of the 1,778 library nonusers who were interviewed, less than 10 percent were in school or another educational program.) At the same time, there is a need to respond more fully to the predominantly youthful character of the existing user population and to enlarge upon the school/library relationship which is clearly the major basis for library patronage.

The continuing emphasis on print materials by branches in low-income areas may not be the most effective way to achieve broad-based support among their constituents. First, as noted, the principal variable that distinguishes library users defines only a small proportion of the target population. (This is true partly because individuals with these characteristics are more likely to be upwardly mobile and to move out of ghetto areas as rapidly as they are able.) The evidence suggests, however, that even with these individuals libraries may have to change their programs and activities substantially if they are to assist larger numbers of people in achieving this goal of upward mobility. Multimedia collections and community-based activities would continue to attract current patrons and should attract new users with similar interest patterns and prospects for mobility.

In addition, there are differences between racial and ethnic groups which may require differential programming. Both white and black library users are more likely to be active, curious persons, to know more about the community and its resources, and to be more interested in expressions of the human spirit through music, art, and artifacts. For blacks, however, income also appears as a discriminating variable; the implications of this are uncertain, but for whatever reason, poor blacks are unlikely to be library users. It may be that, for the very poor, the fundamental pressures of survival are so great that the resources of the library as presently constituted are not and cannot be perceived as relevant to the satisfaction of these immediate needs.

For Spanish-surnamed users, the perception of the library as a friendly and helpful place is more important than any other factor in discriminating between users and nonusers. Some Spanish-speaking residents come from countries without public libraries and have no preconceived image of or experience with library purposes or services; their use of the library, therefore, depends almost entirely on the extent to which the library is able to communicate its empathy and its ability to assist them, in particular in overcoming the language barrier.

3 Library Services in Relation to Community Needs and Resources

IN THE community view the library operates as a local institution delivering certain specific services. The kinds of services that a particular branch or library system may provide will differ from city to city; however, there is a fairly well-defined spectrum within which libraries customarily operate, and which includes services in the categories of education, information, culture, and recreation. Table 5 expands these four basic categories to reflect a range of needs and of services responding to these needs which may characterize a particular community. This list was assembled from a review of the literature reporting on activities for the disadvantaged currently operated or planned by libraries.

THE RELEVANT OTHERS

It is apparent at once that the library is not the only community agency delivering services in these categories. In the area of teaching and related services the schools are clearly the primary resource. Poverty agencies frequently assume responsibility for providing information and referral. Both public and private groups may offer cultural and recreational programs or progams intended to motivate interest in learning as a meaningful experience.

To assess both community needs and available resources to meet these needs, representatives of public and private agencies with interests or involvement in the fields of education and information were interviewed in each of the fifteen cities. A semistructured

Table 5. Community Service Needs and Examples of Public
Library Services That Might Be Offered to Meet Them

Need	*Services Offered*
Teaching and related services	Tutoring Remedial reading/literacy After-school study center Preschool programs Adult education
Motivation	Programs to encourage: Interest in learning Parental support for children's educational development Communication between various groups in the community
Educational resources for self-education	Print and nonprint materials Easy-to-read materials, self-learning texts, etc.
Cultural enrichment	Music, dance, theater, art, photography
Community information and referral service	Community center for meetings Information and referral center
Provision of educational materials to other agencies (individual schools, training programs, etc.)	Books and other printed materials Audiovisual materials Programmed learning materials

interview form was utilized with individuals representing, as nearly as possible, persons in comparable positions at comparable institutions from city to city. The prototypes of these subjects may be described as follows:

The director of a multipurpose poverty center or agency located in or operating in the selected branch neighborhood

The principal, or assistant principal, and/or school librarian of a public school in the selected branch neighborhood at a level, e.g., elementary or secondary, appropriate to the program being studied

The principal or librarian from a private school serving the neighborhood

A representative of the city government at the highest policy level at which general familiarity with library programs also exists.

The numbers and types of agencies that were actually visited, and titles of personnel interviewed, were as follows:

Poverty agencies
13 OEO-sponsored agencies or centers
2 private social service centers

Public schools
12 elementary schools'
3 secondary schools

School personnel interviewed:
12 principals
2 assistant principals
3 school librarians

Private schools
10 elementary schools
1 secondary school
1 elementary/secondary school
2 preschools

Of these schools, eleven were Catholic, two Lutheran, and one nondenominational.

School personnel interviewed:
12 principals
2 school librarians

City government agencies
Personnel interviewed:
2 mayors
2 assistants or deputy mayors
1 city manager
2 assistants to city managers
2 city departmental heads
3 assistants or deputies to departmental heads
1 county budget commissioner
1 city councilman
2 city aldermen

The semistructured interviews with these individuals focused upon the following subjects:

Respondent's perceptions of priority community needs (from

the list in table 5) and categories in which public libraries could serve effectively

Respondent's knowledge of public library programs and activities

Working relationships of respondent's organization or agency with the public library

Respondent's perception of overall public library goals

Facilities available through the respondent's organization for: school libraries (schools only); information and referral (poverty agencies only); and financing library programs (city government only).

PERCEPTIONS OF PRIORITY COMMUNITY NEEDS

All of the community agency representatives, together with branch librarians, chief city librarians, and members of library boards of trustees, were asked to inspect the list of needs and desirable services shown in table 5 and to state which of these needs were, in their opinion, the major ones for their communities. The responses were as follows:

Service Need	Number of Times Cited[1]
Teaching and related services	69
Motivation	38
Resources for self-education	35
Cultural enrichment	24
Community information and referral	23
Provision of educational materials to other agencies	21

There is a clear consensus that the greatest need is for teaching and related services. As may be observed in figure 2, the ranking of these needs is roughly the same by all institutions—libraries, other educational agencies, and noneducational agencies. All institutions rate direct educational services as the top priority, with service needs for self-education and motivation close together in second and third place.

Representatives of these community institutions, including li-

[1] The total is greater than the number of individuals interviewed, since some individuals responded in more than one category.

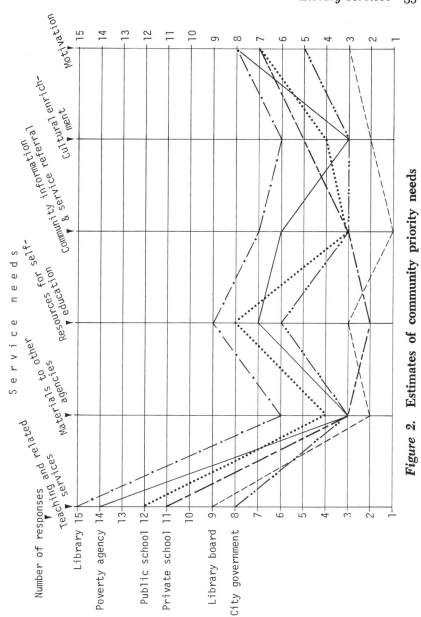

Figure 2. **Estimates of community priority needs**

braries, were also asked to list all of the service categories, e.g., education, information, recreation, or culture, in which they believe that public libraries could serve effectively. There was a general tendency for subjects to respond that libraries could serve effectively in any of these areas. The large number of positive responses received in all categories obscures identification or discrimination as to where libraries might be most effective. What is more revealing about these responses are the negative remarks, the exceptions and limitations upon library activities in certain categories, which were offered by some respondents.

Most of these comments concerned teaching and related services and expressed doubts about whether some or all of the activities suggested in this category are appropriate for libraries. In six cities the library board of trustees expressed doubts about these services, and in eight cities library staff had some qualifications to suggest, the major one being that libraries should offer only facilities and materials in support of an instructional program. It is interesting to note that only three public schools and three private schools objected to public library operation in an instructional program. In the area of cultural enrichment, however, several schools did raise some questions about library service, particularly the effectiveness of libraries in presentations of black or other ethnic culture. There was also a feeling that the arts—music, dance, etc.—were more appropriately served elsewhere. Four poverty agencies objected to libraries functioning in an information role.

Despite these comments by other community institutions, libraries raised more objections than anyone else to the question of how effectively they might operate in these service areas. Doubtless this is due in large part to their superior understanding of the difficulties of working in many of these areas. The point, however, is that opposition by other agencies to libraries working in common areas is relatively low. To some degree this finding contradicts commonly stated judgments that other agencies would protest or object if public libraries moved into some of these common areas.

AVAILABILITY OF OTHER RESOURCES

The study examined the availability of other community resources to meet needs in two categories: education and information.

Education. All of the twenty-nine schools visited were asked sev-

Table 6. Selected Characteristics of Public and Private Schools

	Public Schools	Private Schools
Total number of schools visited	15	14
Number of schools having a school library	11	9
Number of schools with full-time professional librarian	6	1
Number of school libraries by size of book collection:		
less than 4,000 volumes	–	7
4,000–6,000 volumes	3	1
6,000–8,000	4	–
8,000–10,000	–	–
10,000–12,000	2	–
Unknown	2	1
Number of school libraries with access only during school hours, or for a few minutes before or after school	10	9
Number of school libraries with nonprint materials (records and film/filmstrips)	6	7
Number of schools by student body:		
less than 200	–	7
200–499	2	4
500–799	7	1
800–999	2	2
1000 and over	3	–
Unknown	1	–
Number of schools by grades		
preschool	–	2
K–6	5	1
K–7	1	0
K–8	2	4
1–6	4	0
1–8	–	3
7–8	2	0
7–9	1	0
9–12	–	1
1–12	–	1
2–8	–	1
4–8	–	1

eral questions about their schools and their school libraries (see table 6). Five private schools and four public schools, or 30 percent of the schools, have no libraries at all. Although twenty schools have libraries, only seven of them have a full-time librarian; the rest are open only part-time or use teachers, aides, or parents on a volunteer basis. Most of the school libraries have a number of volumes approaching the standard of 8–10 per child; altogether, the schools with libraries possess 87,000 volumes and serve 12,400 children; 2,800 children are in schools without libraries.

Accessibility, however, is severely limited. Typically, an elementary school child will have access to the library only once a week, in a scheduled class period. All elementary libraries but one are open only during school hours, and secondary school libraries are open at most for fifteen to thirty minutes before and after school. Only one school library out of all those visited stays open until 5 P.M. Thus the resources of the school libraries, which frequently include records, films, and filmstrips, as well as books for school-related work and for pleasure, are virtually unavailable to the student after school or on weekends. Obviously, the school library as a place in which to work, an after-school study or homework facility, is similarly denied to the student.

In addition to this limitation of services and accessibility, there is little integration or coordination of school and public library resources. Of the twenty-nine schools, ten had cooperated with the public library in some sort of joint project other than the standard class visits, but in eight of the ten cases this cooperation was for a one-time activity such as an art exhibit, children's book week, or the like. Twenty-three of the schools operate special educational services or programs for disadvantaged students, but only five of these have had formal support or materials from the public library. Only two schools, both private schools, reported any joint projects involving materials, although several indicated that they had in the past utilized classroom collections from the public libraries. It appears that this practice has declined as school libraries have been built up, frequently with federal funds.

Twenty-two of the schools indicated that there would be an active interest on the part of the school administration in cooperative projects with the public library, and fourteen schools indicated specifically the kinds of additional resources that they would like to see the library acquire. The private schools generally would like various kinds of audiovisual equipment and materials; as may be seen in table 6, they are typically much smaller than the public schools, and their limited resources obviously cannot allow them to purchase much. Other schools asked for more materials on black subjects, easy-to-read materials, and Spanish-language materials. Five schools said they did not know enough about what the public libraries already had to comment on additional materials.

The standard class visits to libraries and librarians' visits to schools have served reasonably well to acquaint the schools and students with library services and programs. Nineteen schools feel that students are at least adequately informed of library programs and services, and the same number state that the school staff is kept informed of library programs and services.

However, the existence of these channels for communication does not seem to have facilitated effective coordination; the picture that emerges from this review of schools' relations with public library resources is one of wasteful duplication and relatively unused collections of print materials in both the school and the branch libraries, plus almost total lack of planned working relationships to facilitate priority goals. Accepting the practical constraints that might limit joint planning in the area of primary instructional source materials, there is still clearly a vast area of second-level priority needs—for self-education and motivation—in which school/public library interaction could contribute by careful joint planning to reinforce and supplement educational objectives.

Information. The availability of community resources for information was examined in the study in the context of adult needs for information of a practical nature in health, family management, employment, education, current social issues, and similar subjects. As noted in the preceding chapter, significant unmet needs exist: Large numbers of both library users and nonusers are not informed of community resources and are ignorant of existing community services.

This information function, to the extent that it is being provided at all, has been largely assumed by the poverty agencies. A number of public libraries perceive this service category as one of their functions, but not more than one or two are attempting to operate actively as neighborhood information centers. For those libraries who might wish to expand operations in this area, the views and attitudes of poverty agencies are of interest. Table 7 summarizes the views expressed by poverty agencies in reviewing their relationships with the library. In eleven of the fifteen cities there has been some contact and joint activity, but only three of the poverty

Table 7. **Selected Characteristics of Public Library Relations as Perceived by Poverty Agencies**

Poverty Agencies	Previous cooperative activity	Joint activity effective	Interest in future cooperation	Poverty agency staff informed of library activities	Poverty agency estimate of					
					Effectiveness of library in informing community of library activities			Library effectiveness as community institution		
					Good	Adequate	Poor	Good	Adequate	Poor
City A	Yes	Yes	Yes	Yes	X				X	
B	Yes	No	Yes	Yes			X	X		
C	Yes	NR	Yes	No					X	
D	No	NR	Yes	NR		NR			NR	
E	Yes	NR	NR	NR					NR	
F	Yes	NR	Yes	Yes	X					
G	Yes	NR	NR	NR	X			X		
H	No	Yes	Yes	NR			X	X		
I	Yes		Yes	Yes		X				X
J	No	Yes	Yes	No					NR	
K	Yes	NR	Yes	Yes	X					
L	Yes		Yes	Yes		X		X		
M	No	No	Yes	Yes		X			NR	
N	Yes	NR	Yes	Yes			X			X
O	Yes		NR	Yes		X				X

NR: No response

agencies thought that the cooperative projects had been effective. Most of the agencies said their staff was kept informed of library activities, but indicated their feeling that general community awareness of library activities was not satisfactory. Individual staff members of poverty agencies were asked to rate the library's efforts to keep the community informed of library activities, with the following results:

Rating	Number of Responses from Individuals
Very good	3
Adequate	4
Poor	7
Don't know	1
No answer	1

Their view of the overall effectiveness of the library as a community institution functioning in the neighborhood is not more encouraging:

Rating	Number of Responses from Individuals
Very good	3
Adequate	3
Poor	5
Don't know	1
No answer	4

All of the poverty agencies expressed an interest in cooperation with the public library on future projects, but the prognosis for success of such projects cannot be too favorable as long as these agencies are not convinced of the value or outcome of such efforts. On the other hand, the user/nonuser data suggest that the agencies themselves have certainly not been able to master the resources needed to meet community needs for information.

FINANCIAL SUPPORT FOR LIBRARY SERVICES

The foregoing discussion has presented the results of the investigation in each community of the service priorities established in that community and of the availability of other local organizations or agencies to deliver services that would meet these priorities. Together these considerations serve to delineate the service categories where the unmet need is greatest and where public libraries might therefore serve most effectively. However, these opportunities for library services can be severely constrained if funding sources are limited. Therefore, in each city appropriate administrative personnel were asked to state their views as to whether their local municipal administration was interested in expanding financial support of library programs for the disadvantaged. In twelve cities the answer was negative; the reasons given cited chiefly lack of funds. Four of these city sources indicated that they would favor expanded library programs for the disadvantaged, but only if this were achieved by a rearrangement of priorities to divert a larger share of current library budget allocations for this purpose. In only three cities did local officials indicate the likelihood of increased local support for these programs. These cities included: (1) a city with independent library tax sources, which are due to rise in the next few years as a result of an increase in millage rates; (2) a city which has traditionally funded library services to the disadvantaged from local rather than federal sources; and (3) a city with a new administration committed to additional services for black residents.

Each of these cities offers a more or less unique situation conducive to expansion of these programs. For the most part, however, the prevailing view of local funding resources must be realistically viewed as negative. Cities face rising social expenditures and shrinking tax revenues, and libraries must compete for these decreasing funds with the police, fire departments, and other city services. At the same time, library systems must meet rising costs of materials and wages with annual budget increments merely to continue to offer the same level of service.

Thirteen of the fifteen cities visited have received federal financial aid for services to the disadvantaged, eleven from Library Services and Construction Act funds and two from other federal programs. It may be noted in this connection that all of the programs except one that appeared to have achieved some measure of success in reaching their objectives in service to the disadvantaged (several of these are described in chapters 6–10) had received very substantial federal support, approximating $100,000 per year or more in each city. The support is sizable not so much in dollar terms as in relation to local resources that might be mustered for the same purpose. In one city, for example, the demonstration branch has a budget two to three times that of other branches, and it is doubtless generally true that federal funds make possible an investment in a particular program unit—a branch or a special program—that the local system could not possibly afford to allocate from its regular budget.

It may well be that a relatively large dollar expenditure is essential for visible program impact in ghetto areas, in which case local library systems will be obliged to depend even more critically upon federal assistance in this area. Yet federal aid is also limited, and to secure it libraries must be increasingly competitive in terms of justification and results.

4 Problems in Decision Making and the Need for Evaluation

THE PREVIOUS chapter has described the information that was gathered concerning priority community needs. In some way, obviously, public libraries must be able to take account of these needs and reflect them in their programs and services. This chapter proposes a conceptual tool, an approach to planning and evaluating programs, which was used by the study team in its appraisal of the fifteen selected programs and which a public library can readily adapt for planning and self-assessment.

In recent years there has been a steady growth of federally financed social programs. This has been followed by the development and refinement of systematic principles and techniques for administering and managing these programs. Most such management approaches utilize the fundamental premises of systems analysis in a planning, programming, and budgeting system. Program decisions are made in relation to agreed-on objectives and based upon what appears to be the best method for achieving those objectives. The decisions are then reviewed and revised on an annual or other basis as information becomes available on the results.

This process of guiding the program by means of planned decision making and subsequent evaluative feedback is relatively new to the administration of library programs for the disadvantaged. However, it is important and productive, not only at the federal level but at local levels as well. The interviews with city officials suggest that the rising tide of financial crisis in municipal government is likely to threaten seriously the survival of libraries in low-income areas. As program budgeting becomes a more familiar tool at the municipal government level, the program results of libraries will be scrutinized carefully and critically in relation to the cost of the programs. This is even now true when federal sources are looked to for support, since it is a requirement for federal social programs of all types that they be evaluated, that there be some accounting for the money and resources that go into these programs and some fairly clear criteria to guide policy planning and decision making.

EVALUATION FUNCTIONS AND MEASURES

At the federal level, evaluation is intended to inform and guide federal policy making, providing answers to questions such as the following: What broad variables or categories of variables are critical to the success of library programs for the disadvantaged? Which program approaches advance what is known about the nature of learning and effective education for the disadvantaged? What comparisons can be made between projects on a cost-effectiveness basis?

At the local level, a library system should have available feedback on program operations which will produce answers not only to general policy questions but to the management decisions of library programs: Which groups are being reached? How are library services regarded by their recipients? How efficient is the pro-gram operation? Which new activities should be tried? How do actual program results compare with expected results? How well does the program succeed in achieving its objectives?

These kinds of questions cannot currently be adequately an-swered, primarily because existing data collection practices in li-brary systems are not at all addressed to this purpose. Regular reporting continues to be focused on the condition of the book collection rather than on the patrons or the programs. The fifteen library systems were queried as to any impact measures and other program data currently collected, with the meager results shown in table 8. All of the libraries keep records of circulation, and most record participation in special events, but few collect any program-related data on a consistent basis that would be useful for measur-ing the impact of their programs.

This type of analysis does require some measurable outputs

Table 8. Types of Data Recorded to Measure Program Impact

Types of Data	Number of Cities Using
Circulation count	15
Number coming into branch or facility	2
Number participating in activity	10
Other type of user count	4
Requests for services	6
Reactions from individuals, groups, agencies, etc.	6
Involvement with other agencies	3
Follow-up on individual participants	2

or some rough proxy for program outputs, even if they are somewhat unsatisfactory. One reasonable measure for most of the library programs which were visited in the study would be the absolute or relative change in the number of users. Since virtually all of the programs have as one important explicit or implicit objective increasing the number of library users, it is a measure which libraries could (and should) adopt fairly readily. Doubtless one reason why librarians resist counting heads and feel that this "does not tell the whole story" is because for the most part, as will be seen, the special programs have not been significantly successful in achieving this objective. It is argued that program objectives are defined in terms of developing skills and meeting human needs, that these objectives are, of course, most appropriately measured by changes within the individual, and that such types of change are most difficult to measure. However, even if substantial gains were to be demonstrated by each individual participating in library programs, there would still need to be sufficient numbers of users to justify according to some common standard the library program costs. For example, suppose that a library program costing $30,000 per year to operate produces a measurable impact on fifty users. One would need to consider whether the same impact might be produced by some other method for less than $600 per person, or whether $600 per person is a feasible expenditure level for this purpose, in view of other demands or social priorities in the community, even if the impact cannot otherwise be produced.

   Another proxy measure of how well both the quality and quantity of services delivered by the library have satisfied user needs over a period of time is the overall consensus among informed members of the community as to the value of the library's special programs.

How effective is the library program in the view of the community leaders, institutions involved in related programs, and neighborhood residents? The reflection of the public librar ⁷ in the specific community it is attempting to serve—i.e., community awareness of special programs, reaction to the staff and the library system, previous involvement or lack of it with the public library—appears to be a reasonable indicator of the effectiveness of the library and its programs and might be amenable to systematic development and quantification.

It must be recognized that neither number of users nor community attitudes, as measures of success, attack directly the question of how the impact of library services upon an individual can be measured or quantified. This has yet to be developed adequately, and only a start has been made in this study by identifying some of the characteristic needs and interests of users. Not only is it difficult to develop measures of individual gain or change; it is even more difficult, given the voluntary, varied, and informal nature of library services, to develop methods for determining whether such gains or benefits are in fact attributable to the program being studied.

What Was Evaluated. In considering what types of data ought to be developed, collected, or recorded for evaluative purposes, a schematic model of program relationships and possible measures, such as that shown in figure 3, was constructed, reflecting the basic relationships examined in the study. It was postulated that each of these basic relationships ought to approach an optimum state as follows:

1. Program objectives should be related to individual and community needs, i.e., to user requirements
2. Program planning and implementation should carry forward program objectives
3. Program output (results) should reflect the achievement of program objectives and hence the satisfaction of user needs and requirements
4. Program resource inputs (costs) should be appropriate to the level of program output.

In the popular sense of the term, evaluation of a social program is usually considered to be an estimate of measurement of its

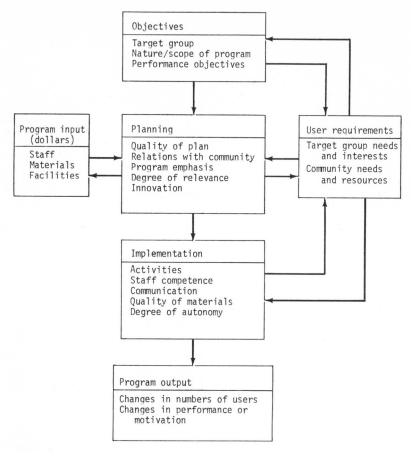

Figure 3. **Library program input/output relationships
and measures**

ultimate effect upon individuals or groups, i.e., the third point above.
In fact, however, a thoroughgoing evaluation utilizes data and
information from many sources to test the validity of all of the
four hypotheses listed above in relation to the program being
evaluated.

In this study, as noted in an earlier chapter, we have utilized
research approaches from both case study and cross-program analysis in an effort to collect the needed information: detailed observa-

tions in each community, findings of structured questionnaires and interviews, and the user/nonuser survey data. This knowledge can then be arranged according to the four categories of objectives, planning, input, and output; and the relationships between these categories analyzed and evaluated.

Use of the Planning Matrix. In reviewing the information and data that were collected in the study, it is obvious that there is wide variation in what was available concerning each of the four points above. Obviously, few library systems were able to provide much of this information, but the study instruments were designed to search out and collect what was available. A prototype for displaying and using this information is shown in tables 9 and 10, which set forth the data collected in two of the cities visited. An administrator might use such a matrix to trace the relationships of program inputs, from the setting of objectives through planning and implementation, to program outputs and to measure loosely program effectiveness.

The first three columns of tables 9 and 10 describe the program being studied. Column 1 lists the program objectives, in terms of scope of program and target groups, gleaned from formal statements or informal understanding. Column 2 lists all of the activities carried out as part of the program during a given period, and column 3 lists program costs for that same period, usually a year, showing the allocation of these costs as among staff, materials, and facilities. Columns 4, 5, and 6 then set forth the study team's evaluation of the basic program relationships as they apply to each project. We see an evaluation of objectives in terms of relevance to community and individual needs in column 4, and in column 5 an evaluation of planning and implementation in relation to objectives. Column 6 lists available information on program outputs. The fourth relationship, that of costs to output, can be determined by comparing the cost data in column 3 with the information in the evaluation columns 4–6.

Theoretically each activity should be shown with its own costs and its own evaluation measures. It would then be possible to make decisions as to the relative merits of different kinds of activities within one program. It would also be possible to look at one kind of activity, meetings or discussions on political subjects, for example, as carried out in several branches or in different library systems, and to make some comparisons as to costs and impact.

Table 9. Program Planning Matrix, City K

Dollar Input (Annual) Percent Going to							Evaluation
Staff	*Material*	*Facility*	*Total*	*Objectives*	*Target Group*	*Activities*	*Objectives*
72	23	5	$120,000	Service to Spanish-speaking communities	All Spanish-speaking, especially adults	Special collection, 40% Spanish	Clear
				Emphasize cultural heritage		Holiday social events	Clear
						Inter-preting for Spanish-speaking individuals	Clear
						Consultant services to groups interested in Spanish materials	Clear
						Special programs related to topical issues: grape strike, brown berets	Clear
						Scholar-ship to graduate library work for Spanish-speaking	Clear

Evaluation

Planning	Implementation	Appropriate to Community Needs	Appropriate to Target Group Preferences	Output Measures Circulation	Users	Other
Good	Excellent	Yes	Provides relevant materials	Up from 24,000 in 1966 to 54,000 in 1969	Adults in proportion to general population. 80-90% Spanish-speaking	Contacts with numerous groups for consulting, joint projects, etc.
Excellent: other groups contacted	Good	Meets affective needs	Yes			
Spontaneous	Good	Provides needed service	Yes			
Good	Good	Provides needed service	Request from many groups			
Good: cooperation with other groups	Good	Issues important to community	Yes			
Good	Good	Very few Spanish-speaking librarians	Rewards achievement			
All staff Spanish-speaking	Yes	Yes				

Table 10. Program Planning Matrix, City E

Dollar Input (Annual)   Evaluation
Percent Going to

Staff	Material	Facility	Total	Objectives	Target Group	Activities	Objectives
76	16	9	$160,000	Upgrade educational achievement, solve problem of unsafe streets	Grade school children	Bussing grade school children to library	Broad
						Mobile units bring books to grade schools	Clear

The planning matrix can also be used to develop some general comparisons and commonalities among total programs which could be particularly useful at state or national levels.

One example can be developed from table 11, which shows a matrix incorporating condensed data from all fifteen cities. When we compare dollar inputs, i.e., costs, with the evaluation ratings, level of funding seems to have some relation to program effectiveness. Five of the programs were funded in the $30–40,000 range, and none of these have been totally successful. Some of these had problems in design or implementation, but even the excellently planned program in City A reached a very limited number of participants. Generally speaking, this level of funding will support only one or two staff people plus some materials and equipment, a level of operation which is apparently not large enough to show an economic return for the investment. Obviously size alone is not a factor, since several of the programs with large budgets did not succeed any better. However, the more effective programs do tend to be those operating on a larger scale. About $100,000 per year,

Evaluation

Planning	Implementation	Appropriate to Community Needs	Appropriate to Target Group Preferences	Output Measures	
				Circulation	Users
Poor: not enough attention to all aspects	Poor program content, poor tie-in to school work, no busses available after school	Provides needed service	Solves safety problem but not relevant materials, no provision for affective needs	Circulation up from 35,000 in 1968 to annual rate 90,000 1969	95% school-age children
				450 children bussed per week	
Good: co-operation with other agencies	Good	Provides needed service	Not known		

for example, will generally support a differentiated staff of eight to fifteen people (including some part-time workers), and a group of this size can bring an array of competencies and a large number of man-hours to a program.

One conclusion, as noted, is that economies of scale are realized in larger programs, with higher benefits and lower per capita costs than small programs. This harks back to the point (p.46) that if per capita costs exceed some given limit, perhaps alternative uses should be considered for the money. Another related conclusion may also be implicit: It may be that, in the context of current program planning, producing an effective program for the disadvantaged is like putting up an office building or a steel plant—it is just not possible to complete without a large investment of resources. Perhaps some sizable minimum annual outlay is required if a program of services to the disadvantaged is to have effective impact within the neighborhood or service area, reaching a sufficiently large number of community residents to keep per capita costs at an acceptable level.

Table 11. **Program Planning Matrix, Fifteen Cities**

Dollar Input (Annual)

City		Staff	Materials	Facilities	Total	Objectives	Target Group
		Percent Going to					
E	Branch/ Program	76	16	9	$161,000	Upgrade educational achievement	Elementary school child
J	Branch					Traditional service to community	All
	Program	38	36	26	$200,000	Users thru outreach New materials for Spanish-speaking	All Spanish-speaking
L	Branch					Users/relevant materials	All
	Program	65	24	11	$110,000	Educational materials to groups	Organizations acting in basic education
C	Branch	69	21	10 (est.)	$ 85,000 (est.)	Traditional service to community	All
G	Branch	57	24	18	$ 40,000	Traditional service to children	Mostly children
	Program	76	24	0	$ 40,000	Outreach/users	Children
N	Branch	65	25	10 (est.)	$ 60,000 (est.)	Outreach/interest programs	Young adults
	Program				$ 80,000	Library use/programs materials	Inner city all
A	Branch	75 (est.)	17	8 (est.)	$ 20,000 (est.)	Users/better materials	All
	Program				$ 35,000	Improve personal development of teenagers	Teenagers

Activities	Objectives	Planning	Implementation	Evaluation	Evaluation	Output Measures	Output Measures
				Appropriate to community needs & other	Appropriate to target group preferences	Circulation (and percent increase from previous year)	Users/Other
Bussing classes to library, mobile units	clear	good	poor	yes		3x over previous year to annual rate 90,000	450 children per week
Weekly film for children						6% to 97,000	16,000 program participants
Aides in branches, programs, special materials	broad clear	good	good	yes			40,000 new books per year added to collection
Films, teen group, and special programs	broad		good		yes	5% to 40,000	
Distribution of materials	clear	good	good	yes	Presumably yes		30,000 volumes per year distributed to public
Clubs, films, facilities to groups	clear	good	good	yes	yes	9% to 85,000	
Movies, art materials	clear					1% to 34,000	
Special programs, mobile unit, films	broad						
Games, clubs, special programs, films (numerous)	broad	good	good	yes	yes	106,000	
Aides, materials, advice to branches, bookmobile, and deposit stations	broad	good	good	yes	yes		
Book discussions, films, special programs	broad					Down 40% to 8,000	
Photography	clear	good	good	yes	yes		100 participants

(continued)

Table 11.   (**Continued**)

Dollar Input (Annual)

City		Staff	Percent Going to Materials	Facilities	Total	Objectives	Target Group
K	Branch/ Program	72	23	5	$120,000+	Service to Spanish-speaking/ emphasized	All Spanish-speaking/especially young adults
O	Branch	72 (est.)	13 (est.)	14 (est.)	$ 90,000 (est.)	Traditional service to community	All
	Program	70	15	15	$ 60,000	Outreach to nonusers	All
H	Branch	60	28	12 (est.)	$ 15,000 (est.)	Service to community	All
I	Branch/ Program	54	12	34	$ 80,000	Meet local needs	All
F	Branch	70	20	10 (est.)	$ 75,000 (est.)		All
	Program	50	50	—	$ 30,000 (est.)	Relevant services	All
D	Branch					Relevant services	Children & young Adults
	Program	52	23	25	$ 35,000	Job materials to disadvantaged	Adult poor
M	Branch/ Program			0	$ 35,000	Service to poor	All poor
B	Main library				—	Traditional service to whole city	Whole city
	Program				$ 1,700	Service to disadvantaged	Disadvantaged

Dollar costs are from the latest year for which financial data are available. Some figures are from the current fiscal or calendar year, and others are from the previous year, so that the data are not strictly comparable from city to city. In several cases cost data have been estimated on the basis of staffing levels plus estimates for facilities and related operating costs.

| Activities | Evaluation | | | | | Output Measures | |
	Objectives	Planning	Implementation	Appropriate to community needs & other services	Appropriate to target group preferences	Circulation (and percent increase from previous year)	Users/Other
Special programs, consulting	broad	good	good	yes	yes	4% to 54,000	
Preschool, films, puppets	clear			no	no	6% to 123,000	
Preschool, mobile units, aged	broad	poor	poor	no	no		13,000 (annual rate) participants
Reading program for school children	broad	limited	adequate	yes		Same at 55,000	
Clubs, films	broad	poor	adequate poor	no		Annual rate 20,000	
Preschool, films, facilities to groups	broad	poor	limited			20% to 30,000	
Special programs/ mobile units, deposits	broad	adequate	adequate		no	4,000	
Games, art materials, preschool	broad	poor	poor	yes	yes	15% to 30,000	
Deposits in poverty agencies	clear	poor	poor		no	Average rate 700 per year	
Films, special programs	broad	poor	good		yes	12,000	4500 users
1 bookmobile stop every 2 weeks	limited	limited	good	limited	limited	2,700 this year	

Output data similarly represent statistics from the most recent year available, which varies from city to city. Also output data may not coincide with cost data for the same city, since the reporting period may differ.

5 Program Objectives and Implementation

IN EACH of the fifteen cities visited, the study team came with detailed, structured questions about the nature of the special program for the disadvantaged which had been selected for study. These questions sought to elicit the information required for analysis, as described in the preceding chapter. This information included not only a description of the program in terms of personnel, activities, facilities, etc., but also an understanding of the strengths and constraints of the program and its role in relation to community needs. In order to form evaluative judgments concerning program objectives, implementation, and their relation to individual and community needs, answers were sought to questions such as the following: "What are the objectives of the program? How were they determined? What is the relationship of this program to other library activities at branch and system levels? Where is the focus of decision making? How much autonomy does the project director have in planning and implementation? What group is the program designed to serve? Who are the participants, and are they representative of the neighborhood? What has been the level and nature of community participation and involvement? What kinds of methods or techniques does this program use in order to communicate itself to the community?"

Table 12 shows in detail the information relating to library programs that was included in the program data instruments in each city. On the basis of these data, together with the interviews with representatives of other institutions in the community, interviews

Table 12. **Summary of Program Data Collected in the Field**

I. Program goals
   A. Target group
      1. Demographic and socioeconomic characteristics
      2. Special characteristics
      3. Relation of current target group to that specified in original plan
         a. Changes from original plan
         b. Changes proposed but not made
      4. Program participation
         a. Numbers in program
         b. Recruiting methods
   B. Nature of program goals/objectives
      1. Most important, if more than one
      2. Any changes suggested since original plan
      3. Any differences in short-range/long-range goals
      4. Participation of outside groups in choice of goals

II. Program implementation
   A. Emphasis
      1. Materials vs. outreach focus
      2. Participation from outside and importance of outside involvement
   B. Activities
      1. List of all current activities
      2. History of program activities since original plan
      3. Program logistics
         a. Frequency, hours, duration
         b. Suitability of location
      4. Decision making re choice and implementation of activities
      5. Public relations and promotion
      6. Relation of program with branch
   C. Resources
      1. Resources allocated to program
         a. Materials, print and nonprint
         b. Equipment
         c. Facilities
         d. Staff
            i. Requirements for staff positions
            ii. Recruitment methods
            iii. Perception of library role by staff
            iv. Perception of community needs by staff
      2. Decision making regarding resources
      3. Dollar costs
   D. Organizational effectiveness
      1. Staff meetings, other internal communication
      2. Cooperation with branch
      3. Decision making
      4. Orientation or in-service training
   E. Impact measures
      1. Current measures
      2. Suggestions for new measures

(continued)

Table 12. (Continued)

III. Other programs within the same branch serving the disadvantaged
    A. Goals, objectives
    B. Activities
    C. Target group
    D. Resources
    E. Staff
    F. History of programs

IV. Routine branch operations
    A. Materials
       1. Print and nonprint
       2. Loan of materials to schools
    B. Staff
    C. Impact measures
    D. Organization
       1. Decision making
       2. Organizational relation to program and rest of system
       3. Participation of outside groups
    E. Public relations

V. Other programs within the system serving the disadvantaged
    A. Goals, objectives
    B. Activities
    C. Target group
    D. History of program

with residents, and informal observation in the field, the study team was able to take measurements, in a figurative sense, from a variety of positions and thus to obtain an overview and assessment of the program in terms of the four basic program relationships referred to in the preceding chapter (p.47). The program data in particular were most useful in assessing the first two of the four basic relationships: the relevance and appropriateness of program objectives, and the quality of program planning and implementation. The balance of this chapter discusses these two major questions in detail.

ASSESSING PROGRAM OBJECTIVES

One of the fundamental questions examined in this study is what the goals or role of the public library in the community should be. Traditionally the role of the public library has centered upon the collection and distribution of printed materials, a functional definition which parallels the traditional definition of the public school as an institution for instructing children in academic subjects.

The current educational crisis, particularly in urban areas with disadvantaged populations, has required public schools to assume conceptual and practical responsibilities beyond providing children with academic knowledge. Public schools, as well as other community agencies providing broadly educational services to the poor, have undertaken an obligation to meet wide-range human needs. Libraries can do no less if they are to remain as viable institutions in low-income urban areas. And libraries are, in fact, willing to take on a new and broader role. In this study library staff and community agencies were asked to state what they considered to be the major role of the public library in their community. The open-ended responses were coded in the following categories (corresponding roughly to categories of community needs and services described in chapter 3):

1. Serves as traditional reference source providing books and non-book materials
2. Provides direct instructional services
3. Provides resources for continuing (self-) education
4. Contributes to cultural enrichment
5. Serves as focus for social interaction
6. Serves as community information center
7. Serves as concerned helping/outreach agency.

Tables 13 and 14 show the distribution of responses in these categories. There are definite differences in the perceptions of these objectives, with library staff generally willing to accept a wider range of functional roles than is attributed to them by the community. In every one of the fifteen cities the library is seen by other community agencies as a traditional reference source but is perceived as having potential for a broader role in less than a third of these cities (table 13). When individual, rather than agency, responses are totaled up (table 14), 50 percent of community responses cast the library in a traditional reference role, whereas only 25 percent of library staff perceive this to be the major library role.

It is clear that while many libraries have been willing to move beyond the traditional areas, most communities have not discerned these new roles. The role of the public library as perceived by the

Table 13. Number of Cities in Which Various Goals Are Perceived as Major Library Role

Goals	By library staff	By community institutions
1. Traditional reference source	14	15
2. Direct educational services	9	5
3. Resources for self-education	11	9
4. Cultural enrichment	6	5
5. Social interaction	6	2
6. Community information center	9	4
7. Concerned helping/outreach agency	10	5

Number of Cities in Which Goal Perceived as Major

community remains a function not necessarily related to community needs. Although community agencies accept in the abstract the idea that libraries can work in new or broader service categories (p.36), in fact, the communities have not noticed or responded to library program efforts in this direction.

Perhaps one reason for this failure is that the libraries themselves have had difficulties in translating these broad goals into workable program objectives. Expressed program objectives frequently iterate purposes such as the following:

1. Meet the needs of community residents
2. Improve delivery of services
3. Improve communication with community
4. Develop more relevant and appropriate activities.

Aims so stated do not permit the design of activities, the benefits of which can be measured against goals. Libraries with general and undiscriminating statements of purpose were more likely to have difficulty than were those libraries that had already arrived at specific objectives. For example, "provision of relevant educational materials to groups working with the disadvantaged" is a goal permitting method of design and is, in current terms of librarianship, measurable. One of the troubling aspects of some of the nonconventional library programs that were visited is that the library personnel themselves have difficulty in defining specific objectives and seeing where the program leads to. What do cooking

Table 14. Role of Public Library in Community as Perceived by Library Staff and Community Institutions

Numbers of References by Individuals

City	Library Staff							Community Institutions						
	Traditional reference source	Teaching and related services	Resources for self-education	Cultural enrichment	Focus for social interaction	Information center	Helping/outreach agency	Traditional reference source	Teaching and related services	Resources for self-education	Cultural enrichment	Focus for social interaction	Information center	Helping/outreach agency
A	3	2	1	1		2	2	2	2	1	1		1	1
B	2	2	2				2	4		3	1			
C	3	1	1			1	3	2	1	1	2		2	3
D	2	1	1		1	3	2	1						
E	2	2	2		1			3	2	2		2	2	
F	1	1			1			4						
G	1		1			1	1	5		1		2		
H	2					1	1	5						
I	1		1	1				3		1				
J	1		1	1				4			1			
K		2	2	1	1	1	1	1		2	1		2	2
L	3	2	3	2	1	2	2	2	1	1	1			1
M	3	1	2	2	1	2	3	3		1				
N	3					2	1	3	1				1	
O	1							2						
Total (number)	28	14	17	8	6	15	18	44	7	13	6	4	6	7
Total (percent)	26	13	16	8	6	14	17	50	8	15	7	4	7	8

Total number of library responses: 106

Total number of community responses: 88

classes or creative dramatics have to do with libraries? The answer may be, in some cases, nothing, unless these activities have been carefully structured in terms of program objectives.

The preceding chapters have indicated a clear consensus in virtually all communities that teaching and related services supporting formal educational achievement constitute the major community need and focus of concern within the range of a library's services, for all of the agencies queried. The community resources currently available to meet this need and to meet adult needs in subject areas such as health or job information are clearly not adequate. At the same time the major findings of the user/nonuser survey indicate clearly that library use in low-income areas is currently limited primarily to participants in formal educational programs. Thus specific program objectives aimed at supporting formal educational achievement—not only for school-age children but for adults in educational and vocational training—would have the virtues of building on existing patterns of use and responding to priority community needs.

The nature of libraries as education-oriented, yet voluntary and informal institutions, suggests that their efforts should be aimed both at building cognitive skills and at meeting affective human needs. Therefore, programs should be planned with both of these basic dimensions in mind. Programs designed to enhance cognitive skills may include not only those directly related to reading and print materials but functional competencies encompassed in the concepts of individual growth and self-education. These include the ability to acquire and communicate ideas, the ability to reason logically, and personal and environmental competence in areas such as physical and mental health, citizenship, family life, and occupational skills.

ASSESSING PROGRAM IMPLEMENTATION

After the data shown in sections II–V, table 12, had been collected in each city and the programs evaluated by the study team (see chapter 4), the cities were grouped roughly into two, with the better programs in one group and the less successful in the other. Then the information gathered concerning various aspects of program implementation—program emphasis, program activities, resources, etc.—was analyzed to determine whether there were patterns characteristic of either success or failure.

Some of these program factors seemed to make little or no difference in program outcomes. For example, it seems to make no difference whether programs focus on materials or on outreach activities; examples of each turned up in both successful and unsuccessful programs. On the other hand, certain major programming factors did emerge from the aggregate of individual profiles as contributing critically to program success or to program failure. Although the programs visited represented a cross section of geographic location, size of city, target group, and type of population, certain common aspects of program strategy appear to play a dynamic role in success or failure in virtually every city. For the most part, these factors are generally applicable to all types of programs and, most importantly, are within the control of the program developer or administrator. The balance of this chapter discusses the topics covered in the outline (section II, table 12) under "Program implementation," presenting selected findings concerning those factors regarded as the most important determinants of program outcomes.

Emphasis. The materials vs. outreach issue was not found, as noted above, to be related per se to program success or failure. On the other hand, participation by outside groups was found to be essential to program success and its absence associated with less successful programs. Thus participation needs to take the form of genuine community involvement and support. Successful programs are characterized by solicitation of community views and implementation of these views, by the existence of shared projects, and by the presence of individuals personally active in both library affairs and community affairs. In addition, successful programs sometimes find it necessary to enter into the arena of negotiating interagency support; i.e., the library participates in an active community issue in order to gain support for its concerns and ultimately wider use from other groups and individuals.

Unsuccessful libraries tend to overlook the *two-way* implications of community involvement. There may be talk of carrying services "into the community," but this usually turns out to be a one-way flow, from the library to the community, and lacking in the necessary interaction. Community groups need to be involved in planning and in implementation, and they need to be kept continuously informed and reminded of the library's role and of its potential.

Activities. Characteristics of successful program activities include the following:

1. Evidence of the importance of the activity to significant adults in the community
2. Active participation by the target group
3. Emphasis on audiovisual and sensory stimuli as well as print materials.

A major and perhaps essential characteristic of a successful program or activity is that it be perceived as important by adults in addition to those in the library. Even if it is designed for children, the activity should have some community status. In some cases the importance may derive from the topic, such as drugs, Vietnam, birth control, and the California grape strike. In other cases the status of the activity may derive from that of the adults who are involved in it, such as the participation of teachers, clergy, and doctors in a series on sex education for teenagers. The adult leading the project also confers status upon the program by the importance he places on it, as in one city where the children's librarian invested substantial effort in assisting children to polish their creative writing and submit it to magazines for possible publication. In all of these cases the status attached to the activity, and the attention and interest given to it by important others, enhance the participant's feelings about himself and his motivation to sustain or increase his level of participation.

Another characteristic of successful program activities is direct user participation. In programs visited, teenagers participated in selecting films; a teenage council planned social affairs; young adults learned the art of photography by doing and experimenting; children told stories to the librarian; grade school children learned to cook in a fully equipped kitchen. In all of these cases the role of the program user is active rather than passive. He plans; he acts physically to do or create something, which contributes importantly to satisfying affective needs.

When the activity does involve participants primarily as spectators, they respond best to sensory stimuli. Presentations involving art, music, dance, or theatre are almost universally successful. On the other hand, book talks, lectures, and routine storytelling hours are less effective in stimulating audiences to pursue further developmental activities on their own. The importance of sensory stimuli can be seen in the media preferences of library users and nonusers, which reflect a far greater utilization of audiovisual than of printed materials. There is also great reliance upon personal direct communication between individuals as a source of knowledge and information, rather than upon impersonal media of any sort.

Project visibility is a key aspect of program activities. In less successful programs the promotion of project visibility in the community tends to be underrated, intermittent, and carried out chiefly through occasional newspaper items and a seasonally decorated bulletin board. The most successful projects are characterized by unremitting efforts. If a library is to generate the kind of word-of-mouth advertising it desires, it can no more cease advertising than can the local department store. Also, promotional efforts must be tailored to the institution in the community the library desires to reach, with appropriate and creative methods of communication.

Resources. Of the resources available to a program—staff, equipment, and facilities—staff competency is the absolute sine qua non. No amount of community support or of extensive materials or lavish facilities compensates for naive or poorly qualified program administrators and program staff. The requirements for a competent and qualified staff include not only professional qualifications related to library functions but also identification with the community and the capacity for leadership and negotiation.

The presence of professional qualifications is not guaranteed by a library degree. In virtually all library systems visited a library degree is a requirement for professional positions beyond entry level, so that almost all professionals in positions of program responsibility have either a library degree or its equivalent in experience. However, the professional talents actually required for adequate staffing of programs serving the disadvantaged include:

A grasp of programming, i.e., designing and implementing activities appropriate to the target group
A thorough knowledge of materials, both print and nonprint
An understanding of interpersonal relationships
A certain amount of creativity in the performance of job duties.

Beyond these initial qualifications, and they are just the beginning, the staffing need most frequently sensed by libraries as critical is identification with the community. To provide this identification some library systems have hired young people, either idealistic recruits from the middle class or residents of the target community whose, principal (and sometimes sole) asset is an interest in and empathy with the target community. Empathy per se is not enough to attract the interest and active participation of large numbers of individuals. Potential library users are more likely to be moved to participation by the presence of status, of persons of importance and position in the community, persons who are known, admired, and respected. When such persons are hired, they have proved to be very successful in attracting library patronage. As several unsuccessful programs have found, young VISTA types without previous personal or professional connections in the community cannot build a following or promote significant community involvement.

The final dimension of staff competency, particularly important for program directors, is the capacity for leadership, for management, for sustaining the ongoing negotiations, maneuvering, strategies—in short, the politics of program administration—necessary to keep a program flourishing. (It is important to note that the general public does not distinguish clearly the differing ranks of staff members, i.e., professionals, interns, aides, etc. Therefore, it is important that all staff, not just the administrator and key members, be selected with care.)

In addition to staff resources, a program occupies facilities and utilizes materials and equipment. Facilities were found to be a relatively unimportant factor in program operations. Neither convenience of location nor size or condition of facilities in themselves are related to success, apparently, since new buildings and convenient locations were found to be characteristic of both successful and unsuccessful programs.

However, the quality of materials is clearly a vital program factor. Successful programs are characterized by an abundance of well-chosen materials, both print and nonprint. Good materials reflect both an extensive knowledge of the contents of the materials and a very specific and precise understanding of the needs and interests of the target group. Unsuccessful programs, on the other hand, are characterized by standard collections, without a sizable quantity of ethnic materials and without the popular, the easy-to-read, and the controversial items in which people are really interested.

Organizational Effectiveness. The key factor in this area contributing to program effectiveness appears to be the degree of autonomy of the program staff. In successful programs the staff were very much aware of this factor and cited autonomy in decision making concerning staff, materials, and activities as vital for program success. This factor appears most important in larger systems, where the presence of centralized, administrative control and standardized regulations governing all aspects of program operations appears to hamper the development of specialized or innovative services.

Some highly successful programs are so completely dissociated from the rest of the system that, for example, other branches are unaware of the program or of its resources which may be available to them. While this does not affect the operation of the program directly, it does limit the indirect benefits that would otherwise accrue.

Summary. The foregoing has summarized the major findings concerning program implementation. The exigencies of low-income urban society seem to require that most of these factors be present and positive to a high degree; there appear to be among the various aspects of program implementation that have been discussed four or five basic program essentials, the absence of which is not merely a program deficiency but leads more or less rapidly to program failure. These key factors, critical to program effectiveness, include the following:

Competency and effectiveness of staff
Degree of community involvement
Degree of project autonomy
Quality of materials
Project visibility.

In the following chapters, examples from the cities visited have been selected to illustrate the ways in which these key factors operate either to enhance or inhibit program outcomes. Chapter 6 deals with staff competency; chapter 7 with community involvement and support; and succeeding chapters with, respectively, program autonomy, materials, and public relations.

6 Staff Effectiveness

THE CONSTRAINTS of the ghetto environment require much more than the average in program performance; what is not really strong and solid is quickly swept away. The dimensions of staff competency must include not only professional qualifications but also leadership skills, administrative ability, and identification and status in the community. All of these qualities are imperative; programs for the disadvantaged cannot thrive without them. The primary cause of those program failures observed in the field is a deficiency in one or more of these areas of staff competency. Some project directors are professionally well qualified but fail to identify with the community; others are easily and fully accepted but lack the drive for effective leadership.

Although all of the attributes indicated above are essential, the distribution of roles and responsibilities may vary. In one successful program for which the staff had been carefully and skillfully assembled, the director functioned well in an administrative role and had hired one senior staff member to assume responsibility for materials selection and another for community relations. This worked well, and all these functions are being expertly performed. In another city the project director has selected a team of four to handle materials and community relations jointly.

In the city which is described below, staff effectiveness has been built through many years of positive skillful interaction with individuals and groups in the community.

Old Town is a somewhat isolated and self-contained community in one of the oldest parts of City C. The Old Town Branch Library is located on the fringes of the shopping area that serves the neighborhood. This end of Main Street runs through Old Town's poverty area, and here there are few shoppers and the stores are small and relatively shabby. The target poverty area includes three public housing projects and the private housing that lies around them. The private residences, mostly row houses, are old and many are run down; however, they represent a higher standard of housing than the housing projects, which are poorly maintained, ugly, shabby, and have the reputation in some quarters of being dangerous places. Thirty percent of Old Town's population live in these projects.

The number of nonwhite families in Old Town is small; the principal ethnic heritage is Irish Catholic, with sizable Italian, Polish, and Lithuanian nationality groups. Because of its isolation from the rest of the city (Old Town is a peninsula), Old Town has developed into a tightly knit community, resistant to outside pressures and influences. There are strong feelings of pride and sensitivity to the poverty issue. Approximately 15 percent of the families earned less than $3000 per year in 1967, but there are fewer families on welfare rolls than are eligible, and in attitudes and interests it appears that the residents of Old Town identify with middle-class values.

The state has a long history of support to libraries. The fairly recent establishment of City C as part of a statewide regional public library system completed a regional development program, begun in 1960, granting state aid to public libraries and authorizing the creation of new patterns of cooperative library service. The City C Public Library has few special programs for the disadvantaged; its policy is to serve the needs and desires of all residents primarily through the regular programs of educational, cultural, and recreational activities. The Old Town Branch Library was viewed as a typical City C library branch, located in a low-income area.

The library has been in its present location for twelve years, since the building opened. Functionally designed of brick and glass, it contrasts with the surrounding small shops. The main reading room is divided into three sections. The children's section occupies half the library and is separated from the rest by relatively high bookshelves. The remaining half of the library is equally divided for young adults and adults. Children and young adults are restricted to their sections of the library. A large multipurpose room, capable of holding up to 200 people, adjoins the reading room, and for staff use there is a work room and lounge.

Of the branch's 25,000 volumes, over half are for adults, a third for children, the remainder for young adults. There are no comics or easy-to-read adult books. Records may be checked out or played in the library on available head sets. The library is equipped with a movie projector, record player, and piano.

Some of the activities sponsored by the library are story hours, the Junior Book Club, film programs, a Never Too Late group for elderly citizens, and visits to and from schools. The library's meeting room is also available to community groups. There are people in the reading room throughout the day, and attendance at the activities is good. For example, between 30 and 60 senior citizens attend the weekly Never Too Late programs.

The Old Town Branch is totally supported by local funds and has received no special assistance from federal sources. Complete cost data on branch operations are not available, but expenditures on materials and personnel totaled approximately $80,000 in 1969. Of this total $60,000 was spent on staff (5 professionals, 2 clerical), and the rest for materials, almost all of it on books.

The Old Town Branch is apparently successful in meeting the needs and desires of the community. As a traditional branch library, it has status in the community and is considered a contributing, vital institution. Support for these conclusions is evidenced by the continuous flow of users of all ages into the library, by the branch's ability to maintain its relatively high circulation rank within the city system, and by good activity attendance. In addition, if a comparison is made with other low-income libraries (table 11), Old Town's circulation is among the top five of the fifteen branch libraries studied.

There are five full-time professionals on the Old Town Branch staff, the branch librarian and four others. One librarian is assigned to the adult section, one to the young adult, and two to the children's section. The branch librarian and children's librarian have been at the branch for many years, have dedicated themselves to their profession, and have earned the respect of the community. They are the backbone of the library and have given it an atmosphere of stability and the assurance of friendly, dependable service.

Although not a resident of the community, the branch librarian attends meetings several evenings a week, either in an official or unofficial capacity. One of the library users interviewed in the library informed the study team that the branch librarian has entertained the members of these civic organizations (including the respondent) each year at a tea held in the library; the respondent remarked warmly that the latest affair had offered a "beautiful collation."

The children's librarian has equally established a place for herself in the community, with special emphasis on schools, parents, and individual children. For example, for many years she has worked on creative writing with small groups of young children and has scrapbooks filled with samples of their work—poems, stories, essays —some of which have been published in children's magazines. The depth of her concern and her impact on these children was evidenced during the week of the study team's visit when a man who had been one of her youthful protégés some ten to fifteen years earlier and had long since moved away dropped by to say hello.

The branch librarian is responsible for decisions concerning branch activities but not for permanent staffing, which is done at the system level. She has perhaps been fortunate in receiving adequate staff assistance. In any event, she has made a deliberate effort to maximize the contributions of the other three librarians. These three are young women. The branch librarian feels that these librarians often relate better to the young adult patrons of the library. For example, local regulations forbid the library to allow truants on its premises during school hours. The branch librarian has elected to enforce this rule, which might ordinarily have incurred the wrath or alienation of these young people. However, she has tempered the effects of this, not only through her own noncritical way of carrying out this order but also through the presence and activities of the younger staff members and their concern with the peace movement, drugs, housing, and other subjects of local or topical interest to the young people of the neighborhood.

There is an intellectual controversy between the younger and older members of the staff. The younger librarians are a product of the new school of library thought advocating broader interpretation of goals and activities. They would like to see the library take a position on some of the community issues, such as housing. The older members support the traditional system oriented to materials dissemination and educational activity. While these younger librarians have not succeeded as yet in convincing the branch librarian, there is dialogue. The branch librarian creates boundaries for library activities, but the other librarians have a measure of freedom within these constraints.

Community organizations figure as a major channel for communication of library activities. Other advertising methods used to inform the community of library programs are posters in the window, circulars, news items on the radio and newspaper, and school announcements, but the branch librarian considers community organizations, radio, and newspapers to be the most effective.

The librarian believes that acceptance of the library by the community is a valid measure of the library's impact and effectiveness. Not only are the librarians constantly invited to speak or simply to attend community meetings, but there are requests from numerous organizations to place notices of their future meetings on the library bulletin board and to leave leaflets and brochures on various subjects at the library. The great demand for the multipurpose room by community groups, the thank-you notes received by the library for services rendered, and the requests for library services such as new titles or special services to some housing-project residents are also viewed as impact measures by the branch and local library system.

These indications of community support tell a more substantial story than do circulation figures. Old Town's circulation has been declining over the last four or five years, as has that for the city as a whole. However, Old Town has continued to maintain its relative position in sixth or seventh place among the city's twenty-eight branches with a circulation of 85,000 in 1969.

CITY D

As noted above, staff competencies must include professional skills as well as identification and involvement with the community. City D, a small Midwestern city, appears to be an example of staffing where community support has been gained but lack of professional qualifications inhibits achievement of program objectives.

The DeVale Branch is housed in a modest single-family residence which was left to the City D Public Library thirty years ago. Most of the surrounding neighborhood is made up of similar small, older single-family homes, some well kept and others less so. The neighborhood is primarily residential, and there is a junior high school directly across the street. However, there are some small warehouses down the street, and Main Street, one block away, is the main east-west commercial thoroughfare through the city. In 1950 the DeVale house was remodeled, and in 1966 it was enlarged and remodeled again. The more recent remodeling cost $32,000, of which $7500 was supplied by federal library construction funds. The major changes made in 1966 were the addition of an entry, additional office space, new shelves, and tables and chairs. The outside of the building, however, still looks very much like the other homes in the surrounding neighborhood.

Statistics on the racial makeup of the library's target area are not available, but the enrollment at the school across the street from the library is 70 percent black and 30 percent white; these figures probably reflect the general distribution within the immediate area. It appears that the neighborhood is shifting from white to black, and that the black families who have been replacing the whites in the last few years may have lower average family incomes. However, the number of hard-core or welfare families is small. In 1965 the average family income for this neighborhood was $7300, about in the middle of the $5000–$9000 range for City D (county planning commission data); more recent data, reflecting population changes, are not available. The branch librarian characterizes the library's total target area as being 50 percent white and 50 percent black; the city librarian estimated it at 80 percent black. During the November 1969 week of the study team visit, approximately 80 percent of library users interviewed were black.

The staff at DeVale represents a genuine attempt by the director of the City D Public Library to meet the library needs of the community by staffing the library with members of that community. There are no professional librarians; only one person has a college degree (a male youth worker); and everyone is under thirty years old. All staff members are black and include the branch librarian, an assistant librarian, one page, and two "student librarians." In addition, there are two high-school boys, part-time assistants to the youth worker. All three were hired primarily to come in the early evening in order to handle the teenagers who frequent the library after school; they are designated as the staff of the "Neighborhood Library Program." The Neighborhood Library Program was developed by the City D Library System especially for DeVale and another low-income branch, and has as its stated aims to ". . . make these libraries more relevant to the youth who are nonlibrary users and to those who come to the library because they do not want to stay home."

DeVale is one of the few branches which has been able to attract teenagers through the youthfulness, identification, and admirable role models established by the young staff. The youth worker, who earned his way through college, is on the staff of the urban planning office; one of his high-school assistants is a star football player. But what is lacking is sufficient technical resources to turn the library users toward creative and constructive pursuits.

Some of the planned or proposed branch activities include arts and crafts, black history, creative writing, films, foreign languages, field trips, music appreciation, tutorials, story hours, panel discussions, games, and speakers. Few of these, however, have been implemented. This program, for whatever reasons, was not really functioning at the time of the study team's visit. The younger children were coming in to talk and get warm (the principal in the school across the street described DeVale as a "social congregating place"), and many of the older boys were going upstairs to play poker. The "activities" are unstructured, noneducational, and relatively unsupervised. Almost no adults come into the library.

It appears that no one in the branch really knows what to do with the children and teenagers who come into the library. The branch librarian, in her early twenties, is trying to finish college at night. There is a supervisor for the Neighborhood Library Program assigned from the City D main library staff, but this person is also without direct training in this area. Much of the interest that the branch seems to hold for young adults may be due to the fact that an office on the second floor at DeVale is occupied by a City D councilman, representing the ward in which the branch is located. The man is young and black and has moved from a position as an apprentice pipe fitter to a seat on the city council. He is also the director of a local adult education program. His success in local politics and his obvious intimacy with the local power structure, as well as his friendly manner, make him attractive to and much sought after by the young adults who come to the library.

The DeVale Branch has 13,000 volumes, with less than 100 on black subjects, and subscribes to a standard periodical selection. It has about 100 records (mostly classical) and a small collection of 8-mm. films which may be borrowed. These materials are not really appropriate. The book collection is not suited to the community; the black collection is small, there are few paperbacks, and there are no easy-to-read adult books. The branch librarian is aware of most of these shortcomings, but she does not really know how to correct them. She expressed a desire to avoid the whole problem of dealing with adolescents by focusing the entire thrust of the Neighborhood Library Program on a tutorial program for elementary school children, and the city councilman upstairs agrees with her. It is interesting to note that this librarian does not think the major role of the library is to provide book and nonbook materials; its role should be to provide direct educational services, to provide a place for social interaction, and to be a concerned helping agency.

DeVale uses posters, flyers, and word of mouth in its effort to publicize its activities. The flyers are sent to local schools and given to people who come to the library. Most of these flyers are weekly schedules of after-school activities. Yet, as far as the local schools are concerned, the branch library hardly seems to exist. Both the parochial school principal and the public school principal stated that they received little information from the library system, and they had never had any cooperative programs with the branch.

The branch librarian makes few decisions; the branch activities are mostly run through the Neighborhood Library Program (which is itself monitored by the city librarian) or supervised directly by city library staff. The branch librarian did initiate a suggestion that a high-school girl acquire library experience by· working in the library part-time for one semester and receiving school credit for it; this has been implemented.

City D is one library system that does not need to compete with other municipal services for its funds. The three public libraries in the county, of which City D is the largest, benefit from a special county tax which makes about $2 million available to them annually. The county commissioners divide this between the three libraries, and City D usually gets about half. Until very recent years this was a very generous allotment; more recently, each of the three libraries has wanted a larger share than it has received. Because this money is more or less automatically available, there is relatively little motivation for programming/planning/budgeting approaches and similar "hard looks" at program objectives and methods for implementing them; City D's programs would benefit from a challenge either to justify or change their current programming approach.

7 Community Involvement

COMMUNITY INVOLVEMENT and support are vital to program success. True community involvement can be described as both *political process* and *interaction*. It is political in the ordinary sense of the term; the same skills, resources, and continuing effort are required as for achieving any political aim. The process is the coming together of two or more vested interests, each possessed with some power, some "clout," be it political, social, or economic. Where community involvement is successful, the program developer has understood both the potential and the mechanics for entering into working relationships with other groups to accomplish mutually beneficial aims. Where community involvement is not understood, the program administrator may believe, for example, that faithful attendance at community meetings is somehow sufficient by itself to generate the desired results.

In the discussion of program objectives in chapter 5, it was noted that several of the library programs in the study began with goals related to community involvement, e.g., "interpreting the library to the community" or "meeting community needs." Many programs characterized by these goals have failed, and at least part of this failure can be attributed to the fact that the libraries have not fully understood the delicacy and difficulty of the task.

Successful community support requires interaction, two-way channels of communication between people and/or groups, through which joint planning and mutual expressions of interest and advice can take place. The recurring debates in library journals about the concept of "outreach" bear directly on this point. Libraries expect that community support will be generated by outreach, but outreach is often understood and implemented by libraries as a one-way flow, from the library outward. Outreach as a one-way flow does not work; after three years of such outreach by one library, it is still possible at any time during the day to take a nap in the reading room undisturbed until after school hours.

Libraries can and do take their books and other services to locations outside the branch ("into the community"); this is praiseworthy, but it is not community involvement and by itself does not generate the kind of community support that is required. Some libraries have also employed outreach workers. Where the outreach worker is in the mainstream of the social and political life of the community, is a person of some status in the community, and is knowledgeable about who's who and what's what, he serves as a valuable link and source of interaction between the library and the community. However, several cities have chosen as outreach workers young, white, college-educated females, perhaps with VISTA or Peace Corps experience. Despite the talents, creativity, and sympathy of these young women, the possibilities for effective interpersonal relationships between them and the community are often substantially diminished because they really lack adequate personal or professional status. In the absence of that, black communities would prefer to interact with black workers, and Spanish-speaking with the same.

It is not enough, however, to be the right color or speak the right language. Another part of community involvement is the library's ability to accept and respond to social issues of importance to the community, even when these may be controversial. One library, not successful, suppresses Black Muslim literature while another, very successful, handles grape-strike literature as casually as the *Ladies' Home Journal*. Merit, at least in social and political issues, should lie in presenting all sides of a position, especially those the community might be expected to be interested in.

Some of the difficulties of the sort described above appear in the following profile of a branch library in City I. These problems have prevented the library from successfully engaging the support and participation of the community.

BLANDFORD

The Blandford Library Center is located on Tracy Avenue, the main artery of City I's low-income black community. According to 1967 census data, approximately 75 percent of the 8,000 residents in the neighborhood are black, the remainder being white. These black residents constitute about a quarter of the city's black population. Presumably this is the, quarter having the lowest income, since many of them live in public housing. Public housing sets the tone for the neighborhood, even though there are also a number of single-family dwellings and several blocks of attractive new townhouses, well kept and in good repair. The public housing, however, is characterized by litter, broken glass, and vandalism; its high-rise units are considered not entirely safe to enter by other residents of the neighborhood.

The library itself is located on a block without a great deal of foot traffic. In other blocks small storefronts line the street, but in this block the original buildings were presumably torn down in the process of urban renewal. In their place are three or four new medium-sized concrete block buildings with long blank walls, separated from one another by cement and parking lots, and housing the library and a few stores. The effect is not neighborly.

The Blandford neighborhood is well organized. There is a facility or agency to meet every major need, such as unemployment, medical care, legal help, and child care, and most of these agencies have offices in the neighborhood. Further evidence of community organization is the apparent success of the Forrest Community School, a neighborhood elementary school which also offers a number of educational services to the nonschool population.

The library-as-neighborhood-center idea developed in Blandford along with the early plans for the War on Poverty. At that time the city librarian proposed to contribute to the development of human potential by offering a place for encounter, for discussion, and for creative activity which might make up for deficiencies in these opportunities in the homes of the poor. Just as USO centers and portable book collections had formed a refuge for soldiers from the war of 1941–45, it was hoped that these library centers might provide a source of both strength and repose for those who had not yet won their war against poverty.

Specifically, the centers were designed to encourage individual creativity through programs and activities in the library. These activities could be almost anything within the broad spectrum of education-information-recreation-culture, utilizing any and all media and whatever other resources the library had to offer. Each center was to work independently, doing whatever it wanted or viewed as appropriate or meaningful for the community. Although particularly designed to be attractive to the disadvantaged, the center concept was expected to be equally attractive to all library patrons.

The first neighborhood center went well, and others were opened. The Blandford Library Center was planned as the fourth of these neighborhood centers in the City I Library System. The proposal for the Center stated that its single most important goal was to offer a program that would provide neighborhood residents with a range of opportunities to improve themselves and their families by their own efforts. There would be flexibility of program organization and content to meet individual and special needs and desires of the residents, and these needs and desires would be determined by a citizen board known as the Neighborhood Advisory Group. Distribution of books was not high on the list of priorities. The Center opened in 1969, when the building was completed.

The interior of the building, which consists of a main reading room and several auxiliary rooms, is attractive. A uniquely designed story hour pit is located at the rear of the library. The idea for the pit was a good one, but the location is poor. There is no visibility into the pit from most sections of the library, and it has been the scene for many mischievous acts. There is a meeting room with a capacity of fifty to sixty people and a small activity room, with access to a kitchen for preparing and serving refreshments. The meeting room is in great demand and is used almost every night by some community group.

The popularity of the meeting room is not matched by the other services of the library. During the year that the branch has been open, virtually its sole neighborhood users have been children, and so the activities, programs, and services have been mainly directed toward them. Each activity meets weekly for one or two hours under the supervision of a library staff member. There have been a drama club, an art club, a Black Heritage Club, and two cooking clubs. Two additional children's activities are Saturday movies and preschool story hours. A sewing club and book club have been organized for adults. Other library activities for the year included an open house and visits to and from schools, as well as the loan of the library meeting room and facilities to community groups. The immediate objective for each activity was to get a particular target group interested in something that would bring them into the library. The final goal was to get the participants interested in books.

At the time that the branch was visited by the study team, these objectives had not been realized. The number of library users and activity participants was very small. Except for the Saturday movies, no more than eleven people were attending any one activity. The most successful branch activity seemed to be simply providing a meeting place for children of the community. Between the hours of 3 and 9 P.M. about twenty to thirty children of various ages gather to be with their friends. An annual circulation of 75,000–100,000 volumes was anticipated in the proposal; actual figures have been running at a rate under 24,000 volumes.

Circulation count is the only impact measure that is formally recorded at the Blandford Library. Although the Center staff do not consider circulation count to be an adequate measure of program effectiveness, they have devised no other method for evaluating their programs and do not feel that one is necessary. The main library does keep a record of the number of new titles, number of library cards issued, and amount of new equipment. Only the circulation figures from July through December 1969 were available, and they totaled approximately 10,000 books.

In one way or another, failure to involve the community appears to be at the root of this state of affairs. In 1969 the Center held an open house and community meeting with the first Center director as hostess. The turnout of two to three hundred people was very encouraging; however, the director apparently did not relate well to the community, and no one showed up for the second community meeting. The library has avoided confrontation with some of the issues that concern the community. The Blandford Legal Rights Association tried unsuccessfully to get the library interested in legal rights issues, and contends that the staff has never gone into the community with meaningful outreach. Representatives of the Forrest Community School and the major antipoverty agency in the Blandford area had favorable comments about the library; however, neither were aware that the first center director had left (one month after her departure) or knew who was replacing her. Thus these agencies were not up to date on or particularly concerned with library happenings.

The staff as selected by the system does not meet library needs or community desires. The first director apparently alienated some groups in the community; her replacement will have the responsibility of repairing this deficit and creating a positive image for the library. The present new director has not yet moved to this active community role.

In addition to the director, the library staff consists of one other professional designated as a program worker, one paraprofessional, and five clerical workers, four of whom were part-time. The director's duties are primarily administrative; however, she also has functioned part-time as children's librarian. Program planning, community relations, running of the activities, and acting as children's librarian when necessary were the responsibilities of the program worker, assisted by the paraprofessional. Recently a full-time children's librarian joined the staff and relieved the other two professionals in this capacity. The Center director and children's librarian hold M.L.S. degrees, and the program worker has a B.A. degree in an unrelated field. Although the program worker is enthusiastic, sincere, and active in the community, she is a young white woman, recently out of college, and less effective in the community than a black woman would be in the same position. The black paraprofessional assisting her lacks initiative and relevant training or experience. Thus there is no one on the staff with the proper combination of qualifications to attract community support.

Staffing difficulties obviously have their origin at the system level, since all hiring is done at that level. The four neighborhood centers are supervised by a coordinator from the central administrative staff, and this person does not appear to relate to the true concept and implications of the center idea. On a visit to Blandford, the coordinator responded to a group of youngsters who were engaged in mild horseplay with a stern rebuke and the traditional standard of library quiet.

The library has a collection of approximately 20,000 volumes, of which half are children's books. However, only four shelves are devoted to black history and books by black authors. There are very few paperbacks. Blandford receives a conventional list of periodicals, and *Ebony* is the only black magazine. Interviews with educators and community leaders indicate that adult illiteracy is one of the major problems in the Blandford area, yet the branch has no adult easy-to-read books.

The primary purpose of the Center was to determine the needs or desires of the community and to fulfill them. There no longer is an active neighborhood advisory group to define the needs and desires of the residents, and this may be one reason why attendance is poor. Another may be inadequate advertising. Normal attendance for the Saturday movies is fifty to sixty children, but the one week in which additional advertising was used, attendance tripled.

Several activities had to be limited to a small number of participants for reasons of space or equipment, thereby failing to reach many residents who were interested. Instead of accommodating to the limited space by having a number of short-term group sessions, the library schedules a group activity to continue indefinitely and the same people continue to attend until they get bored.

With respect to school visitation and interaction, the library has not succeeded in making its encounters with the children meaningful. The librarian complains that after the story hour only a few children check out books. There are plans for the library to show films for classes in conjunction with their course material, but in performing this service the library will serve only a maintenance function, as it does in lending its meeting room, and the library's potential impact will not be felt.

As noted in chapter 5, it is difficult to plan and execute successful programs when goals are general and potential conflicts or problems not thought through. The first neighborhood center went well, presumably, but the observed difficulties of the Blandford branch have apparently been shared to some degree by the other centers. Now, five years after the opening of the first center, the city librarian questions whether the concept ·is valid and appropriate for libraries, whether this is what people want and need, since they are not responding in hoped-for numbers.

Some of these doubts have doubtless been communicated to the new chairman of the board of trustees, who feels that the problem basically is one of finding out how best to "sell" materials and equipment to the public. He feels that the ultimate concern of the library should be with books and information and not with services that other agencies might be performing.

In 1969–70 the cost of running the first three centers in City I was approximately $120,000, of which about $80,000 was federal money and the balance was from local library system funds. The fourth center, the Blandford Library, was budgeted for an additional

$80,000 for operating costs for 1969–70, of which $22,000 was coming from federal funds and the balance from local funds. No specific data are available as to how this money was allocated; staff accounts for an estimated $45,000, and the balance was presumably used for materials and equipment. This was in addition to the initial capital cost for the new building, which, including land, construction, furnishings, and initial stock of books and equipment, came to $325,000.

CITY O

The experiences of another city, City O, illustrate in a different way the point that has been made concerning the political dynamics of library development. In City O the library system solicited community involvement and attempted to serve what it considered the best interests of the entire community, but in so doing the library created resentment among many black groups. Community negotiation is complex and difficult, as this city found in developments in the Newtown Branch.

The neighborhood which is served by the Newtown Branch is bisected by Royal Avenue, with one side being almost totally black and the other almost completely white. The branch is located on this street. The black area, commonly referred to as the Newtown-Royal area, contains about 8,000 blacks, 80 percent of the total black population in City O. Exact income figures for the Newtown-Royal area are not available, but it is established that most of the families are in the lowest income group in City O. It can be inferred that the white families in the library service area have somewhat higher incomes, since their houses are noticeably nicer than those of the blacks. Most of the residences in both neighborhoods are single-family houses, the exceptions being a few small apartments and a few multifamily dwellings. Both black and white neighborhoods are intensively organized. The area surrounding the library has about 200 community organizations, including 40 churches. Many of these groups, especially black groups, are actively engaged in competition for funding, positions of leadership, and the support of local residents. A number of these organizations have combined in a federation, but the area, as acknowledged in general interviews, remains a highly fragmented community without powerful leaders, in which petty political machinations promote undue turmoil.

The target group for the branch is the surrounding neighborhood. The branch librarian describes this area as being 55 percent white, 40 percent black, and 5 percent American Indian. The purposes of the branch, which opened in 1967, are to provide these groups with books and nonbook materials, answer reference questions, and persuade people to read more. The branch's book and record collection consists of 40,000 volumes and about 500 records, 60 percent of which are classical. The branch receives the standard periodicals, of which three—*Ebony, Jet,* and *Negro History Bulletin*—are geared to black readers. Statistics on the black collection were not available, but what was on the shelves at the time of the study team visit was not more than a couple of hundred volumes. This limited collection is not attractively or prominently displayed. Adult illiteracy is stated to be a problem by the black community leaders, and this is evident in several adult education courses in the area; yet the library has only about thirty adult easy-to-read books. In addition to books, records, and periodicals, the branch also lends framed paintings, 8-mm. films, and pamphlets.

Activities include tours of the library, puppet shows, talks about the library, and movies. Close contact is maintained with the local elementary schools (public and parochial), and the library receives several classes every week. These classes, depending upon the age of the children, take part in a story hour or hear a brief talk about the library, and are encouraged to check out books.

The library is moderately busy throughout the day, with about half of the users being adult. During the week of the study team visit, the sample of users interviewed was 80 percent white, 19 percent black, and 1 percent other.

The building is a former movie theatre that has been completely remodeled, air-conditioned, and carpeted. The result is a modern structure which is comfortable, spacious, and pleasing to the eye.

The branch staff consists of four professionals, two with B.L.S. degrees and two with other college degrees. There are three clerks, four part-time aides, and a Neighborhood Youth Corps worker. All twelve staff members are female, with the exception of two aides, and all are white except for the Neighborhood Youth Corps girl and one of the professionals.

For promotional purposes, the branch distributes flyers and a monthly newsletter (any individual can ask to be placed on the mailing list). Schools are given special attention; teachers receive flyers, they are invited to library teas, and all schools are visited once a year by a librarian.

In general, the Newtown Branch is successful in selecting and providing services to the white half of its constituency. White patrons are attracted from all parts of the city to borrow the carefully chosen paintings, and whites maintain a high level of circulation. Total circulation for the calendar year 1968 was 130,000 and for 1969 approximately 125,000 (a relatively minor decrease in view of the fact that the library was forced, owing to budget restrictions, to close on Saturdays in 1969).

It appears that as long as circulation figures are high, the library is resigned to more or less ignoring the black half of its service area. The branch staff, currently composed mostly of middle-aged white women, has relatively little knowledge or experience of the problems of the disadvantaged. In any case, the black community's attitude toward the library has been shaped by events not under the immediate control of the Newtown Branch staff. In 1963, when a new location for this branch was being chosen, a group of black citizens from the Newtown-Royal area argued that the new branch should be located in the center of the black community. The director of the city library, however, decided that the new branch could serve a wider constituency if it were placed on the edge of the black neighborhood. In addition, the new branch was to be located in the facilities of the local movie theatre, thus eliminating the only neighborhood movie house, which the black residents valued perhaps more highly than the library. As a result of their losing the political fight on location and their only movie theatre, they have had feelings of resentment toward the new branch. These attitudes may have subsided somewhat over the years, but they were recently renewed when a black staff member of the branch, the wife of an activist member of one of the black groups, either left or was asked to leave. Interviews with the leaders of two black community organizations indicate that the library is now not considered a vital or particularly helpful institution by the community.

With two hundred community groups fighting for power, black residents are bombarded daily with outreach workers concerned with identification and solution of their problems. The competition is fierce, and the library, not being an active competitor, is disregarded by both black organizations and residents who are involved in their own struggles. Therefore, the library is not a resource for community action, and its purely educational activities, by means of which it might play a larger role in the area, are not sufficiently promoted in the black community. The black leaders criticize the library staff for lack of effective outreach and for not adequately publicizing library activities.

The budget for the Newtown Branch, one of the nine regular library branches of City O, probably approximates $100,000 annually, with about 65-70 percent going for personnel. The City O Library System faces a problem that affects all users of libraries. City O has been having financial difficulties for the last few years; hence, so has the library. Each year the library's request for funds is cut by the city comptroller to meet the requests of other agencies such as the police and fire departments. A 1969 ballot sought approval for a city surtax which would increase the library budget, but the referendum did not pass. The library system had to close its doors on Saturdays in 1969 because of budget cuts; it is not yet clear what the adverse effects of the 1970 decreases will be.

At least part of the library's financial difficulties stem from its relatively powerless position in the city government. Here again it suffers from noninvolvement with the power structure, this time at the municipal level; the library is consigned to a city department which is traditionally administered by the political "outs."

8 Autonomy in Program Decision Making

CENTRALIZATION OF control is the rule in most library systems, and unfortunately this appears to inhibit programs designed to serve the disadvantaged. Such programs, as we have seen, require staff and materials specially chosen to meet target group needs, and these may well fall outside the standardized guidelines or regulations set up by library systems. It is seldom that a branch or project director has authority to depart from these regulations; the most commonly encountered situation is one in which the branch or project director recommends and "downtown" decides. The project director is usually able to select activities or materials, but rarely does he have control over such a vital element as staff selection. In one of the most successful programs studied, which is described in this chapter, the director had virtually a free hand, and this was cited by staff as a major factor in program success. Autonomy by itself, however, does not guarantee success. In the other program described in this chapter, the director was left to his own devices and the program resources have been largely wasted.

THE SPANISH-AMERICAN CENTER

There are 36,000 people with Spanish surnames in City K. Half of them live in a broad area in the middle of the city with Main Street as its east-west axis and San Juan Avenue bisecting it from north to south (according to a 1966 household survey of City K). The Spanish-American Center is located on San Juan Avenue just

off Main Street. Both of these streets are commercial thorough-
fares; behind them lie blocks of single-family dwellings and small
apartment houses ranging in appearance from squalor to well-kept
comfort. The immediate neighborhood served by the library has
an estimated population of about 15,000 (Selected Census Tracts,
1965). Approximately 30–50 percent of these people are Spanish-
surnamed or of Spanish-speaking descent, and of this Spanish-speaking group, approximately half are at or near the poverty level, according to the neighborhood poverty agency director.

The Spanish-American Center was conceived as an effort to offer
intensified service to all of the Spanish-speaking citizens of City K.
The purpose of these services is, according to a mimeographed
General Statement of Objectives of public library service to Spanish-
speaking citizens, "to acquaint individuals with the various vocational, educational, informational, cultural, and recreational materials
and services which are available through libraries . . . to reacquaint
Mexican-Americans and other Spanish-speaking citizens with their
own cultural heritage . . . and to develop a meaningful service for
the culturally disadvantaged." Special attention was to be given to
adults as well as to children and young adults. The original LSCA
Services Project Application, in discussing the area to be served,
noted that "while the younger school children of Mexican families
may use the library, they (branch libraries) rarely serve adults."

The Spanish-American Center Library opened in 1966 but was
not fully functioning until 1967. The book collection is the heart of
the program; it is completely new and was assembled by the
program staff. Of the 19,000 volumes, approximately 40 percent are
in Spanish. Table 15 describes the collection of books and nonbook
materials, which is clearly an outstanding one. The collection is
doubly valuable, both because of its relevance to the Spanish-
speaking American of today and because it is a pioneer effort in
the field. The requests to the Spanish-American Center for bibliographies and help in assembling similar collections are numerous.
A casual browser is impressed by the range, from popular Mexican
love stories to serious philosophical treaties by Spanish thinkers,
and including translations of classics from Henry James to Curious
George. The lively interplay of the sober and the sportive, with
dashes of the scholarly, is reflected in the periodicals list.

At the time the collection was being put together there were no
bibliographies of popular materials for the Spanish-speaking, and

Table 15. Spanish-American Center Books and Other Materials

Books and Nonbook Materials
Books*

		Number
Fiction (total)	2,000 Spanish	
	2,500 English	4,500
Nonfiction (total)		7,000
How-to-books		400
Chicano history and culture		1,500
Books by black authors		100
Books for Spanish-speaking		4,000
Easy-to-read adult books		1,000
Children's books		4,500
Comics		0
Paperbacks		3,000
Total Books		19,000
Records and Tapes		
Classical music		300
Popular music		1,200
Children's		75
Other		100
Language study		500
Tapes		20

Newspapers and Magazines Currently Received

American Home	El Gallo
Americas	El Grito
Arena	Ellery Queen's Mystery Mag
Argosy	El Malcriado
Arquitectura Mexicana	El Nacional
Artes De Mexico	El Sol
Atlantic Monthly	Familia
Better Homes & Gardens	Fantasy and Science Fiction
Blanco y Negro	Futbol
Box Y Luch	Glamour
Bronze	Good Housekeeping
Carta Editorial	Grafica
Catholic Voice	Harper's Bazaar
Changing Times	Holiday
Chicano Student Movement	Hot Rod
Christian Science Monitor	House and Garden
Claudia	House Beautiful
Columbia	Hoy
Comercio Exterior	Hoy Día
Con Safos	Informador
Confidencias	Inside Eastside
Consumer Bulletin	Jack and Jill
Consumer's Report	Jornal Portuges
Ebony	La Opinión

*Categories are not mutually exclusive.

Table 15. (Continued)

La Prensa	*Popular Mechanics*
La Prensa Libre	*Popular Science*
La Raza	*Post*
Ladies' Home Journal	*Qué Tal*
Lado	*Quinto Lingo*
Latin America	*Reader's Digest*
Life	*Revista De La Universidad De Mexico*
Life En Español	*San Francisco Chronicle*
Look	*Science Digest*
Los Supermachos	*Science Newsletter*
McCall's	*Scientific American*
Mademoiselle	*Selecciones*
Magazine De Policia	*Seventeen*
Magisterio	*Siempre*
Mecanica Popular	*Sports Afield*
Mexican World	*Sports Illustrated*
Mexican-American Review	*Sucesos*
Mexico/This Month	*Sunset*
Modern Photography	*Teen*
Montclarion	*Temas*
National Geographic	*Time*
National Review	*Times of the Americas*
Natural History	*Today's Health*
Neighborhood Journal	*U.S. News and World Report*
New Republic	*Vanidades*
Newsweek	*Vision*
Novedades (Sunday)	*Vogue*
Pageant	

the staff contacted a variety of sources beyond the conventional ones. One such was the Center for Mexican Writers in Mexico, which was very helpful in selecting and acquiring books.

The initial stimulus for the program came from a Spanish-sur-named member of the City K Public Library Commission who had been interested in getting a Latin-American cultural center established. At the time the center idea was being pushed by members of the Spanish community, the library responded to this general interest with a very modest proposal to the state requesting funding for a Spanish book collection. The timing was propitious, since the state library department was interested in a substantial program serving Spanish-speaking Americans, and it prompted the city to revise and submit a much more elaborate and expensive proposal for, in effect, a demonstration branch. This expanded proposal was highly satisfactory to all: The Spanish community was receiving a center, the city library system was receiving an operating branch at virtually no cost, and the state had an opportunity to put into effect some of its ideas concerning a model program for the Spanish-speaking. During the planning stages a strong community advisory board was named, including a woman who is currently the acknowledged leader of the Spanish-speaking community and another who subsequently became the community relations person on the library staff. The latter, the assistant to the director, continues to maintain a direct line of communication to the community.

The city library system has a purely nominal role in the management of the center; since the funding comes from state sources and federal sources channeled through the state, and the director is on leave from the state library staff, major program accountability is to the state and to the constituency.

One way in which the library demonstrates that it is interested and involved in community values is by providing materials and programs on current social issues of importance to the community, even when these may be controversial or the subject of political dispute. For example, the library has joined with other community groups to sponsor open forum meetings on the grape picketing and on the Brown Berets. Other activities and services offered by the Spanish-American Center have included the following:

Some type of observance to mark holidays important in the community: for example, Christmas, May 5, September 16[1]

Exhibits by Mexican-American and other Latin American photographers and artists

Informal classes for Spanish-speaking and for English-speaking groups

Interpretation for Spanish-speaking individuals and groups

Sponsorship of special educational and cultural programs of interest to both the Spanish-surnamed and Anglo communities

Preparation of bibliographies and consultant services to groups interested in materials for Spanish-speaking.

For the last three years the Spanish-American Center, together with other community groups, has sponsored a Christmas *posada*, the most recent of which was attended by about five hundred

---

[1] May 5 commemorates the defeat of Maximilian and the French in 1867. September 16 is the Mexican Independence Day.

people. Other manifestations of community interest and involvement include (1) community fund raising, which in bake sales and similar events has raised $480 so far this year, $675 last year for the library; (2) absence of violence or trouble in the library during its business hours (although there have been two thefts at night); (3) other organizations speaking admiringly of the library's efforts. The funds raised, incidentally, are used in part to buy refreshments which the library makes a point of serving at its special programs and which would not be covered by regularly budgeted funds.

The Spanish-American Center operates more or less independently of the City K Public Library. The program director has complete autonomy in decision making (by virtue of strong state support) regarding staff, which is very unusual, as well as in regard to activities, materials, and services to be offered. As a small example, the Spanish-American Center levies no fines at all, while the rest of the City K system charges five cents per day.

The staff was selected and hired by the director, within the framework of existing municipal civil service regulations. In some cases, such as a Spanish fluency requirement, the director's staffing requirements were more stringent than the city's. In another case the director arranged (with much difficulty) to have the civil service requirements waived in order to hire a desirable applicant. Staffing the professional positions took almost a year, but subsequent turnover has been low.

In the difficult recruitment process, it became apparent that there are very few trained librarians who are also of Spanish descent and fluent in Spanish. Consequently, for the past two years the Spanish-American Center has been offering two graduate study grants of $2500 each to bilingual candidates of Spanish or Latin-American descent.

The library is housed in a storefront building which was designed as a post office and then used for several years as a regular branch of the City K Public Library. Basically, it is a single large room with some screened-off space at the back and upstairs for office and storage. Everything goes on in this room; movies are shown in one corner, records are listened to in another, and newspapers and magazines can be picked up off the racks by the window facing the street. The bookshelves, racks, and tables are undistinguished; a touch of color and luxury is lent by a rug in one area and some comfortable chairs in another.

Most of the library users are adults and young adults, i.e., the major target group for which the program is designed. Mexican-Americans and other Latin-American or Spanish-speaking people constitute 80–90 percent of the library users, as estimated by the director, and represent a broad range of education and income.

Currently the library has a total staff of sixteen, including six professionals, five clerical, and five part-time pages. The professionals are all Spanish-speaking, since this was a job requirement, although only one is of Spanish ethnic origin. Five of the nonprofessional employees are Spanish-surnamed. Thus, at any given time, a library visitor will find at least three or four Spanish-speaking staff members available to assist him.

Of the six professionals, four have library science degrees. These are the director and the three librarians working, respectively, with the collection, with children, and with cataloging and classification. In addition, there is an assistant to the director for community relations whose responsibilities are in the areas of liaison with community, program planning, special events, consulting, interpreting, presentations to community groups, and assistance to groups and individuals in the library. The children's librarian also has an assistant, and there is one more position, currently unfilled, which completes the professional staff.

During the January 1970 week of the study team's visit, the following activities took place:

Monday: Several showings, both scheduled and unscheduled, of a new film, *I Am Joaquin,* based on a poem celebrating the Mexican heritage, to groups of 10–40 people

Tuesday: Spanish- and English-language story hours for preschool children
Visits from a group of about a dozen high school teachers arranged through the board of education as part of a program to educate the teachers about the community

Wednesday: Visit from a group of 25–30 newly arrived Spanish-speaking adults (no English) enrolled in a special skill/education training program
Visit from an ungraded elementary class of about

20 children, mostly Spanish-speaking and some with no English

Thursday: Visit from a class of high school students

Friday: Visit from an elementary school Spanish club.

The visiting groups were received informally. The children watched cartoons in Spanish; the adults saw the new documentary film. There was time for the visitors to talk to the staff, help themselves to coffee and cookies, and browse among the books and magazines before leaving. It appears typical of this library that there is a positive atmosphere, a general air of the library's being used, of something happening, and of informality. It should be noted that most of the library's scheduled activities, informal as they are, are nevertheless geared to support and reinforce formal educational achievement, which, as noted in an earlier chapter, is a top priority in minority or low-income communities.

In addition, there are groups or individuals coming in at any hour to read the well-thumbed magazines, to wait for their friends, to talk to staff members, listen to records, watch movies, have earnest conversations with one another—to do everything, in short, except (a well-worn cliché) use the toilet facilities, since the library does not have any for general patron use.

In addition to its books and other print materials, the Spanish-American Center has made a substantial and successful investment in audiovisual equipment and materials, arranging them so that access or utilization is essentially effortless. There are movies at the drop of a hat, little boxes with filmstrips the children operate themselves, records in open racks, and occasionally classical music played out loud rather than through earphones. There used to be a television set until it was stolen. These things are physically ready to be set up and used at a moment's notice, and minatory signs are largely absent. In addition, the library has a movie projector, slide projector, record player, and three tape recorders available for loan to individuals or groups.

The Center communicates knowledge of its services to the community through a continuous program of public relations, promotion, and advertising. Attractively designed brochures in two languages describe the library; a more or less monthly newsletter is published in two languages and sent out to a mailing list; flyers for special events are dropped at a regular list of twenty to thirty locations, including stores, organizations, colleges, and junior colleges. The local television station, the Spanish-language radio stations, and the Spanish press have cooperated generously in publicizing the library programs. In the view of the program director, media publicity needs to be generated almost continuously, but person-to-person contact and word-of-mouth advertising are the most important. To this end, staff members regularly attend meetings of several community organizations and give talks to student groups, adult education classes, and other special-purpose organizations. The assistant to the director for community relations is a lifelong resident of the area, with extensive organizational and personal contacts in the community.

The success of the library's publicity and public relations work is attested primarily by the comments and responses of others in the community. In this city other organizations were able to respond in great detail to questions concerning their knowledge of library activities or contacts they had had with library personnel. A measure of the library's pulling power through local media lies in the fact that a local theater operator objected to the radio station's carrying announcements of Spanish films being shown at the library, presumably on the grounds that it was cutting into his business.

All of these factors reflect the presence of an unusually skilled and effective staff and of a first-class work effort maintained consistently over a period of time. But primarily they reflect an autonomous organizational structure relatively unhampered by bureaucratic obstacles. As noted earlier, virtually all decision making for the Center is vested in the director, who has the strong support of the state library (which controls the purse strings). Relationships among the Center staff appear amiable and unmarked by tension; staff turnover has been relatively low.

According to the original LSCA Services Project Application, evaluation of the Spanish-American Center was to be made "upon the basis of circulation and reports of library use of materials and reactions of patrons." Subsequently annual reports of the Center have cited circulation figures and reported in a general way on library activities by listing special programs, agencies and organizations with which the library cooperates or has joint projects, meetings and conferences attended, publications, and major publicity efforts.

Circulation figures for the last few years are as follows:

Year	Volumes
1964	40,000
1965	35,000
1966	24,000
1967[1]	42,000
1968	56,000
1969	54,000

Clearly, the program has boosted circulation well above what it was previously. The director believes, however, that circulation is not a good measure of total effectiveness. For example, the Center is now beginning to fill an important leadership role in the state as a source for Spanish-language materials, and "Chicano" materials in particular. ("Chicano" refers to the philosophy and subject matter associated with the ethnic pride and heritage of Mexican-Americans, and particularly those aspects dealing with social change.)

The library receives numerous requests for bibliographies and for help with course materials and selections; neither this demand nor the library's response is reflected in circulation. Many library services to individuals and to visiting groups do not necessarily result in increased circulation, particularly if the groups are from other communities. However, the library has no special method or suggestion for measuring these services beyond listing the organizations. It does not keep count of people coming in or of participants in programs. (The numbers supplied in the sample week's activities mentioned earlier come from observers present.)

The City K Public Library does not have any other programs for the disadvantaged comparable to this one. However, a new branch building is being constructed to serve an all-black, relatively low-income neighborhood, and the City K Public Library master plan calls for a vigorous approach to extend public library services in a comprehensive fashion to meet the needs of racial minorities and the culturally disadvantaged. A staff survey committee has recommended that a departmental position be established for a specialist to supervise the selection and systemwide distribution of books and other materials specially geared to the black community in a program paralleling the Center services to the Spanish-speaking. However, the organizational autonomy of the Spanish-American

---

[1] The Spanish-American Center became fully functioning in 1967. Circulation prior to that date is for the regular branch operation that preceded it.

Center has also created some conflict in the rest of the system. There has been resentment by other branches of the City K Public Library at the relatively large amounts of federal money this program has been receiving.

The program was budgeted for the first two years, 1966–67 and 1967–68, at $150,000 per year. In 1968–69 the program was renewed for a third year with federal funding of $125,000 and local funding of about $20,000 (apparently the city pays the salaries for two positions). In 1969–70 the program was funded with a federal share of $98,000 and a local share of $20,000; this money has been allocated as follows:

Materials	$ 27,000
Staff	85,000
Operating	6,000
	$118,000

In 1970–71 the proposed budget calls for a federal contribution of $97,000 and city funds totaling $65,000. However, there is reason to believe that the federal share may be cut to $80,000, and there is some question as to whether the city will contribute more than its previous annual share of about $20,000. In this event, actual expenditures for 1971–72 would not exceed $100,000.

The Center staff is two to three times larger than that of comparable City K branches, and the materials budget is much larger (a sore point, since in the system very little is allocated for new books). In any event, there has been no real interaction between the Center and the rest of the City K system; the Center director comes to semimonthly meetings of department heads, and this is about the extent of the relationship.

This relative estrangement from the local system has implications for the possible future of the program. There is no real incentive for the system to fund it at anywhere near the current level, since that would be out of line with the funding of its other branches. The City K Library Staff Survey Committee recommended that the program be continued from federal funds, since in that way it would be a valuable service to the population at little cost to taxpayers. There was no recommendation for greater integration within the system.

The Spanish-American Center is noteworthy because it appears to have mastered the extremely difficult trick of serving as a neighborhood center without losing its identity as a library. It is one of the few programs which has succeeded in attracting significant numbers of adults. Perhaps one element in this success is in the stated intention and purpose to serve and attract all of the Spanish-speaking community, not just the poor.

As we saw in chapter 2, the image of the library as a friendly and helpful place and the library's ability to overcome the language barrier are the major variables related to library patronage by Spanish-speaking Americans, outweighing the effects of income, educational level, or participation in a school program. It would appear that the Spanish-American Center has succeeded because it has identified and responded to these specific needs and characteristics of users and potential users. At the same time, it may also be that success is easier for a program which does not set out to serve just the poor or the disadvantaged, but to meet the needs of or provide services that attract a broad economic spectrum of users.

In any case, the usage of library materials and services at the Spanish-American Center observed by the study team, the views and attitudes of other community groups in the service area, and the fragmentary data documenting circulation and other library activities all combine to present a picture of an institution with an established status and vital function in the community and in a larger setting which it has achieved by its own efforts.

ELMWOOD

The story of the Spanish-American Center is a success story; that of Elmwood is not. Elmwood demonstrates that autonomy in itself is not sufficient, without the staff competence and community involvement previously discussed, to produce good results. The director of the Elmwood Project was left to his own devices, without appropriate professional preparation for the job and without adequate community participation to produce a program wanted and needed by the community. The result has been an ineffective program and wasted resources.

The Elmwood Employment Support Project is part of a statewide program developed by a state library for local use throughout the state. The purpose of the program is to reach disadvantaged people with specialized, job-related materials, and to demonstrate to them the relevance of public library services to employment. This particular project is set up in Elmwood, a small city in the Midwest.

A full-time coordinator provides materials for and supervises six small book collections. These collections are located in five community action centers and in the Elmwood state employment office. The coordinator has supplied each of these locations with about 500 volumes and visits each center about once a week. In addition, he supplies material to professional staff at these agencies and has supplied multiple copies of materials to an adult education group. The Project has a mobile van and two movie projectors, which the coordinator uses in the summer to bring films and books to a migrant camp outside the city. The migrant project was developed through VISTA volunteers in the area. Employment Support has also provided books to a summer camp run by an antipoverty group.

The project is managed by a steering committee of the public libraries in the state, but in fact the coordinator has virtually complete discretion in the conduct of his program and the Project is completely independent of any library system, except for the coordinator's occasional meetings with the city librarian. There is no feedback, referral, or sharing of materials between branches and the Project. The Project staff includes the coordinator, a full-time aide, and five part-time library aides hired by the coordinator. The aides work ten hours a week in each of the centers; they are low-income neighborhood residents.

The Elmwood Employment Support Project has utilized circulation figures, occasional user counts, and a questionnaire as measures of program effectiveness. Circulation statistics show a total of 500 books circulated from the six collections during a nine-month period. A questionnaire distributed to the centers elicited fifty returns, in which twenty respondents indicated that they had used the materials in some capacity.

A study team staff member visited two of the locations. At the Elmwood Community Action Center there were four or five shelves of books in the reception area. At the Employment Service office a more elaborate L-shaped arrangement had been set up along one side of the waiting room. In neither site were any of the materials in use at the time of the visits. It is clear that this program does not justify its annual cost of about $30,000. There appears to be no reason to spend that sum in order to distribute and watch over a collection of 3,000 books, with a circulation of 500 in nine months, and to show a dozen movies.

The difficulties of this program can be attributed to many sources, and at least in part to a lack of adequate direction and supervision. The selection of sites in Elmwood was obviously poor, and no apparent thought was given to changing them. The coordinator originally took the initiative in proposing to the state employment agency and the community action centers that they house his materials, but there has been no involvement or in-depth contact with the people whose needs these collections were intended to meet.

The selection of materials consists of many with titles such as *How to Get a Better Job*, *The Art of Job Hunting*, and similar books geared to the world of the high school and college graduate and to the high school counselor, with chapters on how to prepare a résumé and locate occupational information. Placed in an employment office waiting room, these are not books that a disadvantaged person can handle comfortably. More recently the coordinator has added books and films on subjects of particular interest to blacks and some easy-to-read adult books, but this appears to be an example of too little too late. The coordinator is also engaged in a self-initiated project to put card catalogs in each center, with a list of related materials available at the public library. This seems rather a poor idea, since few people with limited reading skills, on their way to a job interview or to secure a needed service, are likely to be interested in browsing through a card catalog. In this project lack of supervision, together with inadequate staffing, has led to program failure.

9 Selection of Materials

THE SELECTION of materials is or ought to be what libraries know most about and do best. Most programs whose objectives have been directly related to books, reading, and materials in print have been successful in assembling and organizing appropriate resources and carrying out their objectives. If programs of this type have failed, it has usually been due to inadequate publicity or promotion, rather than to poor materials.

Despite the number of successes, an equal number of branches still lack even a modest but adequate collection of relevant black, Chicano, or other materials. Many continue to subscribe to a standard list of periodicals which hardly varies from city to city and contains few new or special-interest items.

Easy, free-flowing utilization of the most common nonprint materials is still beyond the grasp of virtually all libraries. The Spanish-American Center, described in the preceding chapter, seemed to be able to turn on a short movie as easily and as naturally as one would pick a book off the shelf, but for most libraries easy access is limited by shortages of equipment and by what seems to be a fundamental disinclination toward audiovisual media. Vandalism and theft are occasionally cited as reasons for not stocking or replacing these items, and this is doubtless a problem. Perhaps if there were more real interest in expanding to other media, more effective ways would be found to maintain the security of the equipment.

The programs that are described in this chapter suggest that the selection of relevant materials requires more than casual acquaintance with what is being published and a genuine grasp of user requirements.

THE READING PROMOTION PROGRAM

The purpose of the Reading Promotion Program (RPP), according to its director, is "to provide meaningful library service to thousands of residents of City L at all age levels who, because of apathy, lack of education, or any of a number of other social and economic reasons, do not make use of existing services. Working hand in hand with other organizations and agencies, the RPP provides materials and services which are enabling the poor to develop and advance themselves culturally and educationally." In practice the program is implemented by providing needed materials to the myriad agencies and organizations that are involved in the education of the disadvantaged in City L, a large city on the Eastern seaboard. Groups, rather than individuals, are the recipients of materials, and these groups act as middlemen between the library and the individuals who actually use the materials. The processing of materials by RPP is kept to an absolute minimum, and it is assumed that the materials will be consumed rather than returned.

The thrust of the RPP, which began formal operations in 1967, is directed toward providing materials for three target groups with differing literacy needs. One target group consists of adults and young adults whose reading levels range from the totally illiterate through the eighth grade. The second group consists of adults and young adults who have attained a reading level of at least ninth grade but who read very little and seldom, if ever, go to a library. The children of the disadvantaged comprise the third group.

The RPP is administered by the Extension Department of the City L Library System. This department is responsible for service to areas outside the scope of the central library and branch libraries. In addition to the RPP unit, the Extension Department consists of the Deposit Libraries and Bookmobile units. It is somewhat difficult to separate the functions of the three units because the activities of the whole department are highly interrelated. The head of the Extension Department is also the director of RPP, and this provides an opportunity to correlate and coordinate the activities of the entire department, thereby reinforcing the resources available for

Reading Promotion. The director is familiar with all facets of the program, and although administrative duties occupy most of his time, he makes a genuine attempt to keep in touch with the organizations in City L that use, or could use, the Reading Promotion materials. Most of the community work, however, is handled by the community services librarian, who is highly regarded by organizations that have dealt with her.

In addition to the director and the community services librarian, there is an acquisition and selection librarian; all three have an M.L.S. degree. There are two library assistants, two clerk-typists, and a driver. There is also a part-time technician who writes proposals, newsletters, etc., but this person is not paid out of RPP funds. Other members of the Extension Department are also involved in the RPP: the children's librarian, the head of deposit libraries, and other members of the clerical staff devote some time to the program.

All of the basic education and literacy materials purchased by the RPP unit fall into one of the following six broad reader interest categories:

1. The community: organizing and planning meetings, civil rights, housing, schools, government, and other similar subjects
2. Family life: consumer education, money management, child care, home improvements
3. Jobs: how to find and apply for jobs: examination books such as the Arco series; and various other job-related materials
4. Reading, writing, arithmetic: all of the materials related to teaching the communication skills
5. Science and mechanics: everything from the natural sciences to how an automobile operates
6. The world and its people: individual and collective biographies, history, geography, travel, culture of the United States and other countries, and history and culture of minority groups. Most of the black literature, which has proved to be extremely popular, is in this category.

Before a new title is added to the collection, it must be approved by the RPP Materials Review Committee. Ninety-five percent of the materials bought for use with the undereducated are paperbound. This policy is followed because paperbacks are much cheaper than hardbacks; groups are more willing to accept the responsibility for paperback collections; paperbacks are more acceptable to the disadvantaged; and most of the RPP material is published only in paperback. The more nontraditional (as far as libraries are concerned) materials are workbooks, teachers' manuals, programmed texts, and mimeographed materials. RPP also purchases, in quantity, periodicals written for adults with low reading levels. One copy of each new selection is placed in the permanent demonstration collection. There are about six hundred titles in the collection at present. Any group wishing to borrow some RPP materials may send a representative to examine the demonstration collection and select the needed materials. RPP sends as many copies of each selection as the group needs within reasonable limits. To date about 90 percent of the organizations using RPP materials have followed this procedure. The collection also contains one copy of each title rejected for multiple purchase by RPP, and a limited amount of material useful to the professional in gaining insight into the educational and sociological needs and conditions of the disadvantaged. In addition to the printed materials, RPP has movie and slide projectors, record and tape equipment, and filmstrips. This equipment may be borrowed for instructional purposes, and during the summer it is used in conjunction with the bookmobile programs.

The study team visited five organizations that are using materials obtained from Reader Promotion. All of these organizations spoke very favorably of both the Reader Promotion Program and the materials that they had received. For example, Wheaton Center, a settlement house, received a small collection about two years ago, and the material is immensely popular. The J. B. Jones Boys' club has a small deposit collection, part of which is RPP material. This collection is popular with grade school children.

The tutorial program at St. Andrews Church utilizes RPP materials in a remedial tutoring program for grade school children. This is one of the few instances in which the materials are being actively used with young children, and the tutor in this program was very thankful for the materials.

In fact, the most praise for RPP came from those organizations that actively employ RPP materials for the purpose of adult education and/or tutoring. An instructor at Oakwood Neighborhood High School, a storefront extension school for unwed mothers, said he had first used RPP materials when he was an instructor in the regular adult basic education program of City L. He found that he could get newer, more relevant, texts from RPP, and he could get them with less difficulty than he could from the City L School Board. In his new position at Oakwood, he was again using RPP materials. Two more instructors in an adult vocational education program also stated that they had first used RPP materials when they taught adult basic education classes, and they had continued to use them in their manpower classes.

While it is clear that the RPP materials were well chosen and extremely useful, it also appears that the project did not get as much credit as it might for its efforts, and there were no indirect benefits accruing, such as increased patronage at branches. The instructors using RPP materials had apparently not shared this resource with other faculty at their schools, since they were ordering them on a personal or individual basis. None of the students at Oakwood or the vocational program knew that their texts and workbooks had come from the library, and they had never heard of RPP.

However, the general impressions gained support the conclusion that the RPP is efficiently planned and implemented, and that the high quality and relevance of its materials ensures their use on a sizable scale, even without further promotional efforts. The project's effectiveness is also attributed by staff, at least in part, to its autonomy in the selection and purchase of materials (although we have seen that autonomy per se does not bring success).

The RPP was set up to be as independent from the rest of the library system as possible, and it remains so. The nature of obstacles that the library bureaucracy might have presented is illustrated by the experiences of one of the branch libraries in this same city, located in a black low-income area. The librarian at this branch is committed to outreach and to action, and feels that the branch programs have been prevented from developing their full potential owing to reluctance of the local system to allocate further funds. He also cites the extremely slow pace of response to requests for timely materials, for multiple copies of popular items, and for publicity assistance. Community issues come and go before the library can be responsive to them, and some, especially controversial ones, the library system is unwilling to respond to at all. The branch head noted, for example, that the central library would not approve subscriptions to Black Muslim or Black Panther papers.

The major drawback, from a program point of view, also stems perhaps from this autonomy; the RPP is not integrated with other library efforts to reach the disadvantaged. The staff at the branch referred to above, for example, knew a little about RPP, but they did not know what kinds of material were available or where most of the materials were being used. Also, as noted above, participants using the materials are frequently unaware that these materials are supplied by the library.

Publicity for RPP has been generated through the use of circulars, the help of the community service librarian, television, other community organizations, newspaper stories, and newsletters to organizations and other libraries. The most effective publicity methods, according to the director, are the newsletters, the community organizations, and the activities of the community service librarian. Other methods have proved to be less effective and/or prohibitively expensive.

The program measures used by RPP have been somewhat limited in scope. One problem cited by the director is the lack of personnel to do follow-ups on collections after they are loaned. Since the materials are loaned to groups, not individuals, it is very difficult to ascertain how much the individual participant has actually used or benefited from the materials. RPP does make an attempt to get circulation reports from groups with collections; the number of people who come in to examine the demonstration collection is noted (somewhat haphazardly); requests for services are recorded; and the titles and number of volumes lent are recorded. The last measure is probably the most accurate (over 58,000 volumes had been loaned to 110 organizations as of August 1969), but it does not necessarily reflect the number of individuals using the materials.

The Reading Promotion Program has been supported by federal funds from its inception until very recently. It was budgeted for $100,000 in 1967–68 and for the same amount in 1968–69. In 1969–70 the budget estimate came to approximately $110,000, distributed as follows:

Personnel	$ 72,000
Materials	26,000
Operating	12,000
	$110,000

Federal funds were available in the amount of $54,000 to support these expenditures until the end of calendar 1969; thereafter City L was obligated to finance the program if it were to be continued.

SANTA MARIA AND PROJECT VIVA

Santa Maria and Project Viva illustrate what happens when materials are chosen without an intimate knowledge of their contents or of the needs and interests of the target group. Here, in a project devoted to providing useful and relevant materials for Spanish-speaking users, the collection has been assembled from standardized sources, by a person unfamiliar with Spanish literature and language, and without planning or participation by the Spanish-speaking community.

The Santa Maria Library is a relatively new branch of the City F Library System, established four years ago to serve a low-income neighborhood with a largely Spanish-American population. The branch is also headquarters for a separately funded project, also intended to provide appropriate materials for low-income Spanish-speaking people in this target area and elsewhere in the city. The project has separate funds and staff, but its director reports to the branch librarian and many of its activities are carried out in the branch.

The Santa Maria Branch of the City F Public Library is situated at one edge of the city, surrounded by seven census tracts in which live one-third of the city's 200,000 residents, almost all of them Spanish-Americans. Half of these families earn less than $2000 annually and live in 70 percent of the city's substandard housing. Sixty percent of the people who are over 25 have seven or less years of formal education (data from "Report from City F," written by a Santa Maria staff member and published in the state library journal).

However, the actual site of the branch is apparently not in the neediest part of this community. The library is located at a main roadway intersection in a sparsely populated section; the surrounding residential area is very spread out and interspersed with empty fields. Few residents live within walking distance of the library, and most patrons would need a car. It can be inferred that the residents living closest to the library are not as poor as others in the seven census tracts from the remarks of the principal of the elementary school closest to the library (two blocks), who estimated that the families of the pupils include no "white-collar" workers but that about 40 percent would be categorized as "skilled and blue-collar workers" with annual incomes of $7000–$10,000. However, the head librarian for the branch believes that the library draws from the entire Spanish-speaking area, and estimated that about 75 percent of those who use the library come from homes in which the annual income is between $3000 and $5000 with only 5 percent earning over $5000.

Housing consists primarily of small, one-story, single-family frame homes. In the area are two large new housing projects operated by charitable organizations on a public-assistance basis for low-income residents. About six elementary schools with grades one through six serve the area, along with a number of Catholic day nurseries and other private kindergartens.

The Santa Maria Branch is modern and airy. The shelves and tables are in one large semicircular room, at one end of which is the children's collection. A community meeting room, staff lounge, kitchen, and cataloging area occupy the rear half of the building, with a separate office for the head librarian. Ample parking space is provided around the building, and a drive-through night depository is provided.

Most of the branch activities and services intended specifically to serve the poor and disadvantaged are channeled through a special, separately funded project that has been operating in the branch for the last three or four years. The major efforts of this project, Project Viva, relate to its goal of developing a collection of books "chosen for high interest but practical reading level with books related directly to the areas of employment, education and daily living" ("Library Services," Project Viva, Community Action Program, *Annual Report*, 1968).

At the time of the study team visit, Project Viva owned over 17,000 volumes. Some of these are used on the Project bookmobile or in its nine deposit collections, but a collection is also maintained at the branch library. The branch has its own collection of 36,000 volumes. There are about 500 volumes in Spanish, from among the two collections, in the branch library.

The Project Viva bookmobile makes stops, usually biweekly, at fifteen to twenty spots. These stops are made in the late afternoon or evening at adult basic education classes, which are held at public schools. Originally the bookmobile had serviced many public schools, but this was discontinued because, as more federal money became available for the schools to increase their own collections, the bookmobile was no longer necessary. However, one school had recently requested that the bookmobile stop there for the children during the day. The nine deposit collections are small and are located in neighborhood centers, churches, and city recreation facilities.

These two services, a bookmobile and the nine deposit collections, have constituted the major ongoing Project Viva effort. In addition, Project Viva has sponsored an assortment of single or short-term activities. When the Santa Maria Branch first opened, there were weekly family movie nights. Rented films were used and books selected for display on the same subject. The most popular films were always those by Walt Disney. Also used were films on travel, sports, history, and consumer education. Attendance at these events fell off considerably over a year and a half, which the Project Viva director attributed to movies being shown more frequently on television. Film evenings are now held at the library about six times yearly. Publicity is through the newspaper, television, and radio announcements.

Dispensable paperback books have been placed as "minideposits" around the city in five or six public gathering spots, such as laundromats and barber shops. While these books do not have to be returned, each is labeled as having been placed by Project Viva, and return to a branch library is suggested.

Storytelling in different contexts has been used as a Project Viva activity. For a while a storyteller accompanied the bookmobile on its evening rounds of adult basic education programs. This was done while the City Recreation Department was running child care hours for the children of adults in the adult basic education classes. The storyteller would engage the children while their parents were going through the bookmobile. However, this was stopped when the Recreation Department discontinued the child care.

During the summer high school students are assigned to the library as a part of Neighborhood Youth Corps and summer employment programs. The three at Santa Maria used their talents to put on a show about three hobos and presented the program to over twenty groups of youngsters in different locations around the city.

During the summer school vacations the Project Viva director, working with the others on the Santa Maria staff, has organized children's activities, including puppet shows and several contests. One of the most imaginative of these contests was between students of the different elementary schools to reach the highest number of *parents* newly registering for library cards.

Despite these activities and continuing interest on the part of the City F Library System, the Santa Maria Branch and Project Viva seem to have been only minimally successful in building a rapport with the community. The Santa Maria Branch is relatively very lightly patronized and is sometimes empty during the day. Circulation, which is the only measure of program effectiveness taken by the staff, shows Santa Maria circulation at about 30,000 in 1969, somewhat improved from 25,000 in 1968. Project Viva circulation figures, for the bookmobile and the nine deposit collections, show a decline from 4,500 in 1968 to 4,000 in 1969.

There appear to be several reasons for the disappointing showing made by the branch and Project Viva to date, prominent among which is a lack of relevant materials. As noted above, there are only 500 books in Spanish among the 50,000 owned by the branch and Project Viva. Santa Maria subscribes to 32 magazines, of which only 2 are in Spanish. The Project Viva director, who has selected his own materials, does not read or speak Spanish fluently, which doubtless accounts for the few selections in Spanish. On one occasion a representative from an antipoverty group complained that the Project Viva books looked like a "gringo collection." The Project Viva director took steps to correct this by asking each agency involved in the city poverty programs to appoint people to a book selection committee. This was done, and the committee met twice, although representatives of only three or four out of eleven agencies attended. The Project Viva director described the books selected by the committee as being "even more gringo" than what they already had. No further follow-up has been done on this problem. The committee idea simply did not hit a point of significant interest, and no other solutions have been tried.

The project director has generally chosen his books on the basis of standard sources, such as *Books for Adults Beginning to Read,* published by the American Library Association, and lists from other publishing houses specializing in adult education. This method of selecting materials is not foolproof. Perhaps the lists do not include what people really want to read or would choose themselves. There is no certainty that such lists include the particular materials used or desired in the various education programs in City F. The bookmobile stops at the adult basic education classes, and the teachers there can steer people to the available materials, but that is where the coordination of library services and the basic education classes begins and ends. Further evidence of lack of insight into the question of materials is the only very recent acquisition of a large number of Spanish-English dictionaries and English teaching records. A recent idea, too, was the purchase of large numbers of paperbacks to be kept in the branch building.

The lack of familiarity with the needs and requirements of intended users appears to characterize not only Project Viva but also other aspects of the Santa Maria Branch operations. The head branch librarian does not see her main function as being the development of specialized programs, activities, and projects for the "disadvantaged" population surrounding the branch. While she is neither opposed to nor really uninterested in such services, her true interests seem to be more in line with her functions as head of book selection for the whole system and as head of a twenty-county library resource program. These responsibilities, in addition to the everyday operations of the branch, simply require almost all of her time and attention. This was confirmed by her own statement that she really was not interested enough in planning new activities to make time in her schedule to do it. In spite of all that was said and written about the Santa Maria Branch's being placed where it is with the thought of making it a branch offering specialized services for a poor Mexican-American population, the head librarian has left the development and operation of specialized services to Project Viva.

When the branch was established, it was expected that the majority of users would be children of school age and younger. While the stated emphasis of the branch is on programs and materials for children, these activities are lacking in imagination and frequency. The continuing activities of any significance are a Saturday story hour with an average attendance of six to fifteen children and routine visits of classes from nearby schools. For the latter, the children's librarian mails out letters to the teachers at the start of the school year, asking them to select a date to bring their classes to the branch. When the class comes, it receives the usual "This is a card catalog . . ." routine. No preparation or participation in planning is solicited from schools or teachers.

In the past the library had received funds as a component of the Operation Head Start program, and the children visited the library regularly. The program for these visits seems to have been carefully thought out. The attention of the children was maintained by breaking them into small groups and changing the activity every fifteen minutes—from hearing a story to seeing a puppet show or filmstrip to looking at books, alternating listening and participation. All of the activities during a library visit were planned around a single theme. However, for reasons not made clear, the funds for this part of Head Start were not reappropriated in the latest fiscal year.

The full-time staff of five includes: (1) the head branch librarian (holding an M.L.S. degree), (2) the children's librarian (who has a B.A. plus some course work toward a master's degree in library science), (3) the Project Viva director (some college work), (4) a circulation librarian (no degree), and (5) a circulation clerk (no degree), plus two part-time bookmobile clerks and four part-time pages.

The head librarian was moved to the Santa Maria Branch last year. Previously she had been head librarian at another branch located in a more affluent section in the city. She is the only one of the five full-time staff members who speaks Spanish (the part-time bookmobile clerks and pages are Spanish-speaking). The Project Viva director, who has been with the project since its inception and does not speak Spanish, has not been able to expand his program substantially beyond the bookmobile and deposit collection, which were going even before the project and branch were opened. He had initiated other regularly scheduled activities but none that in the long run warranted or developed into large-scale continuous operation. A few short-term projects have been creative and popular (the summer programs, such as reading contests, and the story circuit especially), but current activities include little more than the bookmobile and deposit collections.

The assumption should not be made that a successful activity is always a large-scale or continuing affair or even one that is successful year after year. An inner-city branch might operate very effectively through numerous short- or intermediate-term projects. This kind of an operation might be quite sensitive to changing needs or moods within the target population. On the other hand, the Santa Maria Branch and Project Viva seem to have been successful neither in building a rapport with the community nor in establishing an identifiable image.

All of the materials, services, activities, and programs sponsored by the branch and by Project Viva have been developed in a one-way flow, from the library to the consumer. The bookmobile, the deposit collection, and the neighborhood storytelling carry services out to the user but do not stimulate the user to come to the branch. There is no feeling of interaction, of stimulus and response. The effort that is put into attracting users for a particular program, contest, or story hour succeeds in just that short-term return, and there is no feeling of building long-term community involvement and adult library usage. This failure to involve the community adequately in participation and planning of the collection and other activities is reflected not only in the incident with the other agencies but also in study team interviews with two neighborhood schools. Neither of them had any real knowledge of what was available at the branch or of its activities. One elementary school, itself involved in a variety of community services to adults and children, indicated that the idea of cooperating with the library had not occurred to it and had certainly not been broached by the library.

A major asset which has enabled the program to persist as successfully as it has is the support of the library system and of the city government. Everyone involved in the City F Library System—especially those in policy-making positions—is enthusiastic about extending the services of the public library out into the low-income, Spanish-surname communities. The decision to make this a vital part of the whole library system was apparently made when federal anti-poverty funds were originally given to the city. There seems to be a genuine interest in providing good services of all kinds to the poor residents of the city. The city officials give the impression that this is a prime concern of the current administration. The city manager, incidentally, must give final approval to the City F Library System budget.

Excluding funds for Project Viva, the annual branch budget runs to about $65–70,000, which supports a staff of five professionals and six part-time clerical workers, a collection of 36,000 books, a limited number of other materials, and various activities. The Project Viva budget, running at an annual rate of $30–40,000 (of which about half is federal money) supports the director, two part-time aides, a collection of 17,000 volumes, the bookmobile and deposit collections, and the other activities.

10 Effectiveness of Publicity

PROJECT VISIBILITY is a very important and very much underrated program factor. Effective program promotion is an art and requires unremitting attention. Most librarians believe, and rightly so, that word of mouth is the most effective advertising, but they fail to make the skillful, continuing, comprehensive effort that must go into stimulating and evoking all those interpersonal communications. Particularly in big cities, the promotional effort must be intense and precisely aimed; otherwise it may not be able to penetrate the conflicting din of other claims or the indifference that may characterize big-city dwellers. For example, in one of the cities which is described below, it was found that a children's program had been operating its activities and turning out flyers and posters and newspaper articles for three years, yet the elementary school principal down the street had never even heard of it.

Both East Woods and Linden, the two programs described in this chapter, are characterized by straightforward and reasonable objectives, adequate staff, appropriate materials, convenient locations, and a service that would flourish if people were actively and continuously reminded that it was there. In the absence of an intensive public relations program, they have not generated visibility in the community or reached a maximum number of users.

EAST WOODS

East Woods is a decaying urban ghetto in a large East Coast city,

117

City J. In the last few years more and more blocks in East Woods have been abandoned to the rats, the winos, and the drug addicts. In 1960, though, East Woods was not so bad; the population was fairly stable (52 percent in the same house for at least five years), and family-oriented (75 percent living with both parents). The population was about 35 percent Puerto Rican, 15 percent black, and 50 percent white (1960 census data, Community Statistical Services Research Department). Many of the Puerto Rican families concentrated there have managed to support themselves more or less adequately through employment in semiskilled and skilled positions; current estimates of the percentage of families on welfare or at the poverty level range from 20 percent to 50 percent. (Estimates by school principals, who generally have accurate information on welfare families, vary from 20 percent to 35 percent. The project director estimates that half of the families reached by the project are at the poverty level.) There are strong family ties and pressures for upward mobility in many families. Nonetheless, since 1960 the whites have largely departed, and the neighborhood is mostly poor, bleak, and run down.

The East Woods Project was inaugurated in 1967 to bring new library services and programs to the Spanish-speaking population concentrated in East Woods. Working through several branch libraries, the project is intended to provide new materials in these branches, specifically tailored to interest the Spanish-speaking; modify library procedures to enhance usage; and develop ways and means of attracting the attention of individuals and groups in the community through outreach and special community programs.

Thus the plan provides for efforts both inside and outside the library for the effective delivery of enriched and expanded services. Specifically, this plan has been implemented by the selection and purchase of special materials for distribution to the nine participating branches (there are a total of fifteen in the system) and by the hiring of community liaison workers to work in each branch service area and promote library/community interaction.

The community workers are encouraged to select feasible target groups and develop suitable activities. Among those activities which have taken place are the following: storytelling, film programs, puppet shows, and special presentations to groups in schools, community centers, and churches.

The East Woods project is housed near one of the nine participating branch libraries, the Pine Branch, and utilizes an auditorium in the branch building for community programs.

In each of the two years of its operations the project has purchased and distributed 40,000 volumes, making a total of 80,000, of which 52,000 are in English and 28,000 in Spanish. The project has a movie projector, a slide projector, a tape recorder, and loudspeaker equipment; in addition, it has supplied a record player and records to each branch. The project has purchased 500 records and 33 films. Films are a major activity, and there are films in both languages on a variety of subjects.

Although the total number of books and records is impressive, the impact of these purchases is considerably diminished when they are spread over nine branches. One branch receives an average of 5,000 new volumes per year, of which 1,500 are in Spanish and probably do not constitute more than a small fraction of a branch's holdings.

The project has an annual budget of approximately $200,000, which supports a staff of twenty, including fifteen professionals, an audiovisual technician, and three clerical people. The fifteen professionals include the project director, four specialists who are responsible for selection of materials and supervision of the outreach workers, and nine community liaison workers. The last are each assigned to a branch and divide their time between that branch and outreach work in the community. After being hired, the community workers receive an orientation and in-service training that includes two weeks in a branch and a period of observation in community work. They then conduct all project activities and special programs. In addition, there is a "special investigator," a Spanish-speaking male whose principal function is as troubleshooter to deal with discipline problems.

The professional staff was recruited for the most part from regular library staff. The director is of Puerto Rican origin, as are five of the others; four of the professional staff have M.L.S. degrees, eight have B.L.S. degrees, and the rest do not have college backgrounds. All of the nine community workers are bilingual, as are the clerical workers, and the four specialists are able to read and write Spanish.

Program content decisions are made by the project director, based upon requests for service. Other decisions, such as staffing or facilities use, are made at a higher level. The project director also makes recommendations to the library system on materials and equipment. Approximately one-quarter of the annual budget is allocated to materials and equipment, 45 percent to personnel, and the remainder to operating and other expenses.

The director estimates that 80 percent of the program participants are Puerto Rican, another 15 percent black, and 5 percent white. Three-quarters of these people, she estimates, have less than a high school education, and probably half are at or below the poverty level.

Considering the size and bureaucratic complexity of the City J Library System, there is a remarkable scarcity of evaluative data. The project itself keeps a record of the materials it distributes and of the numbers attending the special programs it provides. It also keeps a record of individual and group reactions in the form of letters, newspaper clippings, etc., and the director regards these communications, together with requests for assistance, as an important measure of program effectiveness.

During the first year requests for programs and outreach activities resulted in an increase of group activities from ten in the first month to more than a hundred per month by the end of the year. Attendance at these activities, held in the branches and in their service communities, during that period totaled 16,000, of whom 10,000 were children.

The recorded accomplishments of the project are impressive, and it is very likely that a much greater promotional effort was made during the first year than during the second. In two neighboring elementary schools, the school librarians, who should have been aware of the East Woods project if it had promoted its children's activities intensively, were unaware even of its existence. Visibility and an image in the community are clearly important; it is very difficult to command support and increased patronage of a program if no one knows you are there.

One explanation for this lack of visibility lies in the design of the project, which essentially precludes a strong identity unless an exceptional publicity effort is made. The community workers operate singly through each of the branches and try to stimulate branch or library patronage rather than to promote the project per se.

Another factor lies in the fact that there is relatively little interest in active promotion at the city level. The total city library system has been slow to respond to the needs of East Woods and other disadvantaged groups. In a city with a Spanish-speaking population estimated at close to a million, in a community that ten years ago was already one-third Puerto Rican, it has required the influx of federal funds, and that only in the last two years, to provide these special materials and services. There appears to be a general feeling in the City J Library System that programs for the disadvantaged lie beyond the library's normal activities, at least at the system level, even though poverty neighborhoods account for a significant fraction of the system's service area. City officials in the municipal department supervising library programs are aware of the fact that other neighboring urban library systems are to date considerably more responsive to the needs of the disadvantaged and more active in seeking innovative approaches to dealing with a changing urban public.

The prevalence and ingrained persistence of traditional views of the library's role is reflected in the first annual report of the East Woods Project. The director cited the lack of availability of easy-to-read materials in the branches before the project was initiated and attributed it in part to limited funds but also to the "necessity of providing a well-rounded book collection in each branch." The branch librarian, in discussions with the study team, echoed this feeling that the library should maintain a traditional collection.

The negative results of an inadequate promotional effort can be discerned in the study team's interview with a respondent at the neighborhood poverty center serving the area in which the East Woods project and the Pine Branch were located. The individual interviewed was the manpower director for the center; he and his staff referred people constantly for information and help to many agencies. Not only was he unaware of the project, but he was also totally ignorant of the Pine Branch, which has been in existence in that neighborhood for sixty-five years.

The Project has achieved notable success in meeting some of its objectives. It has, for example, produced the first Spanish-language library brochures and library card application in the system, and the outreach programs have reached many thousands. However, there is no clear evidence as to how these programs have affected library usage beyond the direct participation in the movies and other activities; Pine Branch circulation has been dropping steadily over the past few years, from about 135,000 five years ago to an annual rate of 85,000 during the last six months of 1969.

LINDEN

In contrast to City J, City M is a smaller community in the western part of the United States, with greater centralization of services and facilities to meet the needs of its disadvantaged residents. Here the public library system thought that it might resolve the problem of project visibility in one stroke by locating a very small branch library within the building that houses many of the target area service agency offices.

The Linden Service Center Library is located in the reception area of the State Service Center, in the heart of the city. The State Service Center houses a broad range of services, governmental and nongovernmental, including rehabilitation, employment, social welfare, corrections, apprenticeship, and health. The target area for these services is the urban ghetto which lies just below and beside the downtown business district. Almost all of the city's minority population, which includes both blacks and Mexican-Americans, lives in the Center's target area, and one-third of these families have incomes of less than $4000 per year.

Efforts to get people in the target area to use the previously existing public library branch had not been successful. It was felt that a new location was needed in order to attract users, and the branch library at the Service Center opened its doors in 1967. The new location was accompanied by a shift of emphasis and a restatement of objectives. These objectives were as follows:

1. To take full advantage of the strategic waiting room location
2. To provide materials needed by Service Center personnel to do their job
3. To utilize service center facilities, such as the meeting rooms
4. To plan coordination of library programs with the total Service Center program
5. To treat collection and program in an experimental manner and to replace those that did not succeed
6. To support stated goals of the Service Center
7. To learn from the disadvantaged how the library could be of value to them.

The Linden State Service Center Library is smaller than the usual branch operation. It has only 8,000 books in its collection and functions physically as the reception area for the Center. The available space is furnished with some couches and a table and chairs for joint use of library patrons and State Service Center clients. All library-sponsored activities must take place either in this very restricted space or in some other part of the building.

In this respect the location has turned out to present problems for the library. The library does not have the freedom of the facility, since the manager of the Service Center must approve the use of any rooms for library purposes, must give approval if the library wishes to be open at other than Center hours, etc. As it happens, the present manager of the Service Center is not favorably inclined toward the library, and this has inhibited library program development. For example, the library started a film program for children and young adults. This program grew rapidly in popularity, attracting more than one hundred youngsters weekly. The Service Center manager objected, pointing out that this number exceeded the capacity of the room provided, and the program was discontinued.

The location itself does not appear to be as serious a hindrance as the overall inadequacy of promotional effort to develop permanent support and response in the community. The library has assumed a passive role. Although many people walk into the Service Center daily, only a few really use library services. There has been no attempt to engage Center users actively; instead the library waits for referrals or for patrons to become interested on their own. Most of the users are not new patrons but have shifted to this location from another branch because this one is newer and more attractive.

The materials are well chosen and attractive. The Service Center staff assisted the librarian in selecting the books and nonbook materials which they felt were most relevant to the community and would meet their needs and desires. Over one-third of the books are by black authors or about black history and culture. Spanish culture, books for Spanish-speaking individuals, easy-to-read adult books, and children's books are also well represented. In addition to the usual periodicals, there are a large number of black and Spanish periodicals. Art prints are on loan to users, and there is a relatively large record collection. Of the 830 records available to borrowers, over 60 percent are popular music (rock, soul, jazz, instrumentals, etc.); 22 percent are speeches by prominent blacks and Spanish and African ethnic music. The library has a movie projector, record player, filmstrip and slide projector, and copying machine.

There is one regularly scheduled and popular activity currently being sponsored by the library, and this is a drama workshop. A theater arts major at the local university conducts the classes twice a week. There are other activities and services which the library performs on an irregular basis. These include handling referrals by the Center who have special problems; tutoring children, illiterates, and Spanish-speaking individuals; and supplying Service Center personnel with needed materials.

The staff of the Service Center branch library consists of the project librarian, a part-time library assistant (with a college degree), two part-time student aides, and a clerk. The project librarian devotes herself primarily to administrative duties. She seldom goes out of the library to community groups or other outreach activities on the grounds that, as the only trained librarian and full-time professional, she should be available within the library. She feels that work-study students are too transient to be really helpful, and essentially she feels immobilized. Although it soon became apparent that the Center would not provide a ready supply of library users, little effort has been made to reach the rest of the community. Community support might have enhanced the librarian's bargaining position with the Service Center manager, but little or no effort has been made to gain it. Community agencies were contacted when the branch initially opened, but no continuing contact was maintained. Whatever services the library has performed for another agency have been at the initiative of that agency.

Impact measures recorded by the library include circulation count, circulation to staff, count of library users, Service Center traffic,. and requests. Materials requested by Service Center staff are counted separately. Circulation count, library users, and Service Center traffic are shown below:

	1968	1969
Total circulation, books and records	14,000	12,000
Number of library users	4,300 (10 mos.)	4,700 (9 mos.)
Number of individuals entering Service Center facility	13,000 (10 mos.)	13,500 (9 mos.)

These annual figures flatten out the curve or trend that is shown by the same data when analyzed on a monthly basis. Monthly counts of Service Center traffic have climbed more or less steadily since the beginning of 1968. On the other hand, monthly reports of library circulation and numbers of library users rose during 1968 to a peak in early 1969 and have been declining since then, despite the increasing Center traffic.

The positive aspects of the Service Center library should not go unnoticed. The collection and activities have been designed to meet the interests and desires of the community. The Service Center staff was consulted for book selection advice, and the small collection is composed largely of Afro-American/Mexican-American history and culture, education, and employment materials.

Both of the activities offered by the library—the drama workshop and the film program—have been planned by those participating, with the librarian acting as consultant, and this factor contributed to their success. However, the relatively small physical scale of the branch operation (the average annual budget for personnel and materials runs at about $30–35,000 and facilities are provided rent-free), together with inadequate promotional effort in the community, have substantially limited the impact of the program.

11 Other Problems in Program Implementation

THE PREVIOUS chapters have dealt with critical program factors that are common to many programs and are usually within the control of the library system. When these elements of the program cycle are improperly or inadequately treated, their cumulative impact leads to program defeat. In view of the difficulties and extraordinary efforts required to correct inadequacies and deficiencies in staffing, planning, and implementation and the very few unqualified successes in the field, one might question whether there is, in fact, a genuine potential for large-scale and replicable program successes in public library services to the disadvantaged. It may be, for example, that the complex constraints of poverty and disadvantage are so negative and damaging to human potential, particularly to the capacity for open encounter with new knowledge and experience, that reversal of this damage would require a massing of resources far beyond those any library has yet been able to assemble.

This depressing possibility remains to be fully explored. What does appear to be true is that the grinding burden of big-city hard-core poverty constitutes a severe constraint upon library program operations. In the grim context of diminished self-esteem, street crime and violence, and sprawling blocks of physical deterioration, it is not clear how much any library or educational program can accomplish.

Regardless of whether the target group is black, brown, red, or yellow or whether the program is well designed and staffed, progress becomes even more of an uphill struggle in the presence of institutional constraints, as is illustrated by the two projects described in this chapter. If we are to provide a light at the end of the tunnel, we must work to humanize our institutions. Such oppressive factors as indifferent local government and rigidified library systems still demand elimination. Where these factors are in evidence, they diminish institutional effectiveness, as we shall see below. Even so, as instruments of remediation in areas where social decay is clearly apparent, library service and education will not provide a solution by themselves, despite the responsiveness they are asked to display.

TRUESDALE

The Truesdale program, although carefully designed to meet community priorities, has suffered both from the exigencies of a hard-core poverty neighborhood and from the rigidities of a highly bureaucratic library system.

Truesdale is one of the poorest areas in City E, a large Northern metropolis. The Truesdale section of the city has a population of 125,000, 90 percent black and half under the age of twenty. Estimates by public school officials of the percentage of Truesdale families on welfare or living at or below poverty level range from 40 percent to 90 percent.

The Truesdale area is characterized by block after block of shabby, run-down tenements, by streets littered with trash and broken glass, by stripped and abandoned cars rusting at the curb, and by roving, dangerous street gangs. Two main streets run through the neighborhood: Lincoln Avenue and River Road. Lincoln Avenue was once a broad and handsome residential thoroughfare with a parkway down the middle, where forty years ago middle-class Jewish families dwelt in comfort. Today its center strip is littered with empty liquor bottles and beer cans, and many of the houses are boarded up. River Road, the business street, was irrevocably damaged by the riots in 1964, 1966, and 1968.

Despite its bleak prospect, the Truesdale community struggles to revitalize and redevelop the area. The neighborhood poverty agency, the Truesdale Urban Center, is the active functioning arm of the federal poverty program. Businessmen and private social/civic/religious organizations are represented in another group, the Greater Truesdale Development Commission, formed several years ago to work toward regenerating the neighborhood.

Until fairly recently, the City E Public Library had done little to meet the specific needs of the disadvantaged and played no role in efforts such as those of the Truesdale community. The Truesdale Branch of the City E Public Library, located halfway between Lincoln Avenue and River Road in the heart of the Truesdale community, was regarded unabashedly by the system as the "worst branch in the city." (This opinion was registered by a member of the library board of trustees in a newspaper interview.) When the librarian currently heading this branch was first assigned to it in 1964, she regarded her assignment somewhat bitterly as a backhanded promotion, a bureaucratic strategy appearing to reward her many years of service in the City E system yet in reality saddling her, a black woman, with a hopeless situation. It is only in the last two years, with a change in the top management of the City E Library System, that there has been a change in the outlook of the library and an interest in improving services to the inner city. The initial result of this interest was a federally funded program to remodel the services and philosophy of the Truesdale Branch, basing it on the neighborhood center concept as developed in *Neighborhood Library Centers and Services: A Study by the National Book Committee for the Office of Economic Opportunity* (New York: National Book Committee, 1967).

The Truesdale Branch building, a substantial older structure, was refurbished, although not modernized. The varnished oak furniture and woodwork and the two-story-high ceilings were retained, but the main reading room and the meeting rooms were brightened with new paint and lighting. The entrance is in the middle of the building, opposite the checkout and return desks. The children's area is on one side and the adults' and young adults' on the other side. The meeting and activity rooms are in the basement. The location of the meeting rooms away from ready visibility and supervision by library staff has created problems of vandalism, theft, fights, etc.; therefore these rooms are not used unless an adult is fully available to supervise their use. Even without the meeting rooms, there have been sufficient problems resulting from the presence of drug addicts, drunks, and street toughs in the neighborhood to require the presence of a full-time guard in the branch. This is the only library system visited where a guard was assigned to a branch library.

In implementing the new role of the branch as a neighborhood center, the gradual development of relationships between the branch librarian and the Truesdale community groups led to the clear definition of a common objective—a no-nonsense goal of upgrading the educational achievement and motivation of the school children in the area, with emphasis, as far as the library was concerned, on getting the children to read. The branch's activities therefore have focused on this objective and include the following:

1. Large-scale bussing of elementary school children into the library, during school hours, for talks and programs by a library technician to explain library service and library skills. Elementary classes and their teachers are brought in for an hour, once a week for eight weeks. This program was begun in the spring of 1969. During the 1969–70 year fifteen classes were brought in from eight schools in the fall, and fifteen more are scheduled for the spring.
2. A mobile caravan that visits six inner-city elementary schools (from among those that are not bussed) during the school year. The mobile unit visits the same schools each week, so that children can take out books and return them through the caravan. In the summer this unit has been used to "rove" through various inner-city areas.
3. The loan of the branch facilities (e.g., the meeting rooms) to community groups that operate special programs, such as tutoring, art, and dance, for neighborhood children.

The aim of the branch is thus to provide direct (and traditional) support to the educational achievement of elementary school children, with lesser attention to recreation or cultural enrichment. Between the bussing and the mobile unit, the branch reaches fourteen of the twenty-one elementary schools in the area.

The branch has 40,000 volumes, of which 11,000 are paperbacks, bought in 1968 with federal funds. Of these paperbacks, 7,500 are for children, and the rest, practically all on black history, culture, etc., are for adults. Children's books also predominate in the regular collection, constituting more than half. Nonprint materials are not much used, except for movies about twice a week. The library has records, but they are not displayed and are for use in the library only.

The branch librarian does not have a great deal of autonomy in implementing the program. The staffing for the Truesdale Branch, as elsewhere in the system, is done centrally and within the regulations of the municipal civil service system. The staff consists of seven professional people and the full-time equivalent of eight or nine clerical people, all black and most living in the community. The branch librarian is a veteran of many years in the City E Public Library, tough, determined to succeed, who has worked hard at building community relationships and community respect and status for herself as the librarian. She has been less successful in transmitting this sense of purpose and commitment to her staff. The other professionals have college degrees but no library degrees, and collectively they give the impression of being municipal employees first and human service workers second, bright enough to have made it into the civil service, eager for the security and pay of the civil service, but without special skills, training, or deep interest in working with disadvantaged children.

These and some of the other weaknesses of the program can be attributed in part to the "system," i.e., to program elements that are within the ultimate control of the City E Library administrators. The Truesdale activities, and specifically the bussing program, are carried out within a rigid administrative structure. The presentations to the children reflect the traditional view that the library is not a teaching agency but rather a materials repository, and they lack excitement or a creative learning spark. The study team was not able to visit any session since the fall school session had not begun at the time, but a report in a City E newspaper described the following for fifth graders: "The first page of the large chart . . . read 'Your library, reading center, learning center, service center.' The following pages . . . talked about users' responsibilities ('respect for property, consideration for others, responsibility for yourself') and the various library sections."

There is apparently little motivation for the children to return on their own, and they do not. The branch librarian could recall only one child who identified herself as coming to the library after being in the school program.

The original stimulus for the program was the neighborhood-center concept, but according to the branch librarian, when the "new look" was unveiled there was an immediate tendency for the neighborhood teenagers to exploit any permissiveness with horseplay, vandalism, and unacceptable behavior. The atmosphere now is traditional but not rigid. Children can talk to one another while seated at the work tables, but too much roving around is frowned on.

A major but unspoken reason for the selection of bussing and the mobile caravans as major activities is that many children (and adults) will not or cannot walk to the library for fear of the street gangs. This also explains in part the children's failure to return to the library on their own, even if the weekly programs were highly attractive. Both the Truesdale Urban Center director and a school principal confirmed the dangers of the street gangs, and this is doubtless a real obstacle: The children may be fearful, and concerned parents in any event may prefer not to let them go. Therefore, it is virtually impossible for the library to assess the contribution of the bussing and mobile units to the children's educational achievement/reading ability in terms of the usual standard of increased library use. However, an indirect reflection of the value of this school-oriented program comes from the principal of the public elementary school directly across the street from the library. Because this school is so close, it is not included in either of the programs; the principal, however, expressed the wish that his children could receive weekly visits from the library, as the other schools do.

The views of the branch librarian as to what the goals of the program should be have obviously been formed with, or at least run parallel to, those of other agencies in the community (the Truesdale Urban Center director reflected the librarian's words and her urgency: "The kids have got to learn to read"). The branch librarian belongs to these community groups and goes to their meetings. Perhaps her influence is reflected in the fact that other institutions in the community are specifically aware that when the neighborhood was predominantly Jewish, thirty years ago, the branch circulation was ten times what it has been in recent years. The study team heard this story not only from the branch librarian but also from the principal of an elementary school and from a worker at the Urban Center. These agencies share the librarian's concern that this lower circulation reflects badly on blacks and that something must be done about it.

The meeting room facilities at the library are welcomed by the community since, as the branch librarian pointed out, a lot of buildings were burned in the riots and there are not too many places to meet. The librarian was also instrumental in getting a vacant lot next door to the library fixed up with some playground equipment.

Impact measures are troubling. Circulation is up because each bussed child takes out books, but that is, of course, no guarantee that the children read them. The library keeps records on its circulation, program activities, subjects in which users express an interest, and informal observations by the branch librarian. Circulation in 1967 was 25,000 volumes; in 1968 it was 35,000, of which more than three-fourths were juvenile books. In the first three months of 1969, as a result of the bussing and the mobile units, circulation was 25,000, compared to only 8,000 for the same period in 1968.

The costs of the Truesdale Branch/neighborhood center were funded from federal sources as a demonstration project for one year. A federal grant of about $160,000 was budgeted as follows:

Personnel	$120,000
Books and other materials	25,000
Mobile unit	10,000
Other	5,000
	$160,000

Federal funds are thus covering substantially all personnel and materials costs for the branch; presumably other operating expenses are being met from local system funds.

FARMINGTON

Truesdale is an example of how municipal indifference and bureaucratic rigidity have created further obstacles and frustrations in an already difficult and even dangerous environment. Official municipal indifference, if not outright rejection, can be equally negative and damaging even where library services are finding a receptive and responsive target. The Farmington Branch of City H, starved of resources by its system administrators, is an example of this situation.

The Farmington branch of the public library in City H, a Southern community of 200,000 people, is situated in a pleasant residential neighborhood that is 99 percent black. The library, surrounded by small, one-story, single-family residences, has a target population which is 60 percent blue-collar and semiskilled workers. However, about twenty percent of the neighborhood residents are professional people: teachers, nurses, and managerial level workers. This is decidedly not the poorest section of the city, although

Farmington is the only branch serving an all-black community. The one other small branch located in a poorer section of the inner city operates for only a few hours a week.

The Farmington Branch is not, in itself, a special program; City H has no special program of services available to the poor or to inner-city residents, nor are there any moves being made to initiate new activities or to change thinking about the responsibilities of the library. Farmington was studied primarily as a prototype branch in a black neighborhood in a small, Southern city.

The branch building houses a traditional collection of 17,000 volumes. Forty percent of the books are juvenile because the users of the branch are mostly elementary school children. There are no adult easy-to-read materials and only about 400 books either by black authors or on black history or culture. The branch takes 5 newspapers and 56 periodicals; 3 of the periodicals are intended for black readers. The record collection includes 50 adult records and 25 for children. The record player is the only equipment owned by the branch.

The librarian, who holds an M.L.S., is the only black among the eighteen professionals in the City H system. She runs the branch with the help of one part-time aide, one part-time page, and occasionally a neighborhood volunteer. A Neighborhood Youth Corps worker was requested as an aide but was turned down by the system librarian, as were other requests for additional help, materials, or resources.

The 1968–69 book budget for Farmington was about $4000. For 1969–70 this was cut to $2500. The salary of the librarian is $7500, with $2000 allotted for the two part-time workers. Thus total costs for personnel and materials are estimated at $12,000 for the current year, a sum far below that of any other program visited and apparently below what City H spends on its other branches.

The responsibility for allocation of resources and determination of library and branch policies rests with the head of the library system. He approves funds, staff, and programs. While the city budget commissioner ultimately approves the budget, he relies completely on the recommendations of the director of libraries. Neither one of these people expressed to the study team any inclination to initiate new ideas or to appropriate the resources necessary to make additional services available either in the Farmington Branch Library or to the inner-city residents in general. This lack of support in the administration is basically responsible for the inadequate materials, programs, and resources at Farmington.

Because the Farmington librarian must operate the branch and its activities virtually single-handed, she has necessarily narrowed her scope to include only those people and activities she can effectively handle. The only organized branch activities are aimed at school children from the neighborhood schools. There is a "Reading for Fun" program, which includes stories, games, and choral reading. This is done for a second- and a fifth-grade class that come to the branch with their teachers twice weekly. Thirty other classes from the schools are brought to the branch twice a year. The content of the programs is planned by the librarian. Her aim is to encourage the children to enjoy reading and activities associated with their reading, and to stimulate expression of their own ideas. The branch also maintains small deposit collections at two nearby day-care centers.

The Farmington librarian relies on the schools for most of her publicity and sends them a monthly newsletter. Occasionally she uses spot announcements on the local black radio stations. She feels that this kind of publicity is largely inadequate. Ideally, she would have outreach workers out in the community. At the present time the surrounding neighborhood is largely working-class. The children from the nearby schools coming into the branch with their teachers do not come from homes in which poverty is extreme. Therefore, the barrier of total unfamiliarity with a library and related ideas on education is not a problem here. However, there is movement of the poorer population from the inner city to the Farmington neighborhood, and the branch librarian fears that without resources for new planning and materials, the potential of the library will decrease.

Despite these limitations, the impact of the Farmington branch library measured by total circulation is high, in relation to the size and scale of the branch operation: Circulation of total books, films, and records totaled 52,000 in 1967–68 and also in 1968–69. The branch's success and pattern of use is particularly noteworthy when compared to that of Truesdale: Truesdale spends ten times as much for very little more in the way of activities, services, and level of circulation.

Community organization leaders and some school staff expressed their concern that the City H Library System does little to be of service to the inner-city poor of City H. They are very aware of the inadequacy of the literacy, educational achievement, and employability of the blacks in the city, but recognize the fact that the Farmington Branch, as it is, can do little to help.

The director of the local antipoverty agency was most interested in expanding the resources and services of the library. His ideas were centered on having the library expand its materials from primarily books to television and other audiovisual and personnel resources (i.e., tutors, and outreach workers reading to people in their homes). He believed that the people of City H need a more relevant information resource aimed at general education and knowledge about living. However, the present orientation of the library administration and the consequent lack of resources appropriated for the inner-city library have made any development or expansion of library functions unlikely.

12 Conclusions and Recommendations

THIS STUDY was designed to examine the scope, nature, and effectiveness of public library services to the disadvantaged in urban areas. It was intended to address two basic questions: How can these services be strengthened? How can their effectiveness be measured?

Both of these questions require the identification of certain criteria, desirable program goals or outcomes, against which ongoing services and results can be measured. At the outset of the study it appeared that there was no clear consensus among librarians as to what types of objectives are most relevant and urgent for libraries to pursue, nor was there agreement as to what constitutes a satisfactory measure of effective or high-quality service. Therefore, the method chosen for investigating these programs was a two-phase approach.

In the first phase, each program was evaluated in terms of how well it was implementing whatever goals or objectives it had set for itself and of its relation to the needs and resources of its constituency. Visits were made to each of the fifteen selected sample projects, and in each city extensive structured interviews were conducted with all levels of library staff, from the branch or project level to the chairman of the board of trustees. Data of a descriptive and quantitative nature, including type of activities, target group, materials and equipment utilized, number and type of personnel, costs, circulation, and similar items, were collected. Information was also sought which would illuminate the dynamics of program implementation: the locus of decision making in the project, the nature of relationships with other community groups, the effort to communicate knowledge of activities and generate interest among community residents, competency and effectiveness of staff, and staff attitudes toward the program and the community.

In addition, an effort was made to sample the specific geographical neighborhood in each city in which the designated sample program or branch was operating. Within this neighborhood, structured interviews were held with representatives of groups or agencies in the community whose interests might reasonably be linked to library activities. These "relevant others" included representatives of public and private schools, the neighborhood poverty center or agency, and the city government. The intention was to gain the perceptions of these groups as to priority community needs in the four service areas of education, information, recreation, and culture. (This spectrum of four service categories was developed to encompass the range within which public libraries might conceivably operate.) The opinions of the community representatives were sought not only on where the priorities might be, but also on what other resources might be available within the community to provide these services, and in which categories public libraries might be expected to function most effectively.

In addition to interviewing representatives of community institutions, the study included a survey of the users and nonusers of the library's services. In each of the sample neighborhoods 200 individuals were interviewed—80 library users and 120 library nonusers—and the results recorded in a precoded questionnaire format.

The second phase of the study stepped back from the case-study framework of the first phase to develop a cross-program analysis, comparing programs in terms of critical points in the program-planning/implementation/output process. Thereby it was possible to identify common elements or factors critical to program outcomes and to develop possible criteria and techniques for assessing program effectiveness.

CONCLUSIONS

In the last few years numerous institutes, conferences, seminars, monographs, and articles have urged libraries to new and nontraditional approaches in program planning. Libraries have been encouraged, for example, to cooperate with other community agencies, to hire staff that can identify with the community, and to move beyond print materials. Such suggestions are confirmed or reinforced by the findings of this study, which re-emphasizes in some cases what is already understood but not always carried out.

However, there is an urgency in the current scene which has not been emphasized in previous studies, and which arises from the serious loss of power and prestige by libraries in low-income areas. In the communities in which libraries would most wish to penetrate, where the general level of education and literacy is low, the library service effort is least successful. Here the predominant library users are a small group of grade-school-age children, using the library primarily for school-related purposes and as a place to meet their friends. The presence of adult users, who constitute roughly half of the libraries' clientele in middle-class neighborhoods, decreases, in some black hard-core poverty areas, to less than 10 percent.

The failure of ghetto libraries to attract large numbers and a higher proportion of adults cannot be attributed to any single factor or set of factors. It can be speculated that in the very poorest areas, the damage to human potential resulting from deprivation, callousness, and neglect is so severe that the public library cannot be perceived as relevant. In this case, no amount of resources reasonably within the command of a public library could be expected to reverse this impact. Nonetheless, the major challenges to the public library which emerge from the user/nonuser survey are clearly these: to better meet the needs of existing youthful clientele and to establish the library as relevant and useful to nonusers, particularly adults in black poverty areas.

Before the spread of paperbacks and television, libraries held a monopoly of a relatively scarce resource, namely, hardcover books and other print materials, as a major vehicle for communication of knowledge and ideas. More recently this monopoly position has been seriously eroded. Cheap paperbacks are widely available and can be purchased for less than the cost of processing and lending through the public library. The scarce resources in communication are now the hardware, the audiovisual equipment, and humanizing interpersonal experiences. These are the resources that are valued by the educational professionals, and also the media that serve as the principal channels of communication for community residents.

It appears that the only groups for whom the utilization of hard-cover books continues to be necessary in everyday life or serves as an important source of status and satisfaction are motivated students and highly educated adults. In the urban ghettos there are few of the former and virtually none of the latter. Among library nonusers over twenty-five years of age interviewed in the study only 2.5 percent have college or higher degrees, compared to 9.5 percent of total U.S. population in the same age range (1966 data from *Statistical Abstract;* more recent data might show an even higher percentage of U.S. population with college degrees). Thus, if libraries continue to operate as they have, their total potential for expanding adult users in low-income areas is this target group of 2.5 percent of the population. Unless libraries in ghetto areas can be perceived as important, prestigious, and useful by more than this relatively tiny book-oriented minority, it is doubtful that they can survive as institutions. The increasingly widespread use of systems approaches to planning and budgeting in city governments will begin to focus more attention on relationships between expenditures and results and to reveal disparities between funds allocated and numbers served.

The implications of the user/nonuser data are reinforced by the responses of the community leaders and representatives who were interviewed. There was a clear consensus across virtually all communities that direct instructional services at a very basic level, including reading skills and formal classroom achievement, constitute the major community need and focus of concern for all of the agencies queried. The community resources available to meet this need, and to meet needs in other service areas such as information, are clearly not adequate. Of the thirty schools visited, 30 percent did not have libraries, and of those who did, only 7 schools had full-time librarians. School libraries are invariably open only during school hours, and since student use of the library is generally restricted during the school day, the accessibility of the school library is severely limited. There is little or no coordination between school and public libraries, no joint planning or even marking out of areas of interest, with the result that there exist, in many communities, waste and duplication of resources which are under-utilized.

Community resources for the dissemination of information—the kind of information on health, child care, job opportunities, and ethnic culture which contributes to the environmental competence of the individual—are also inadequate. About half of the residents interviewed are ignorant of service agencies operating in these areas or of other sources they could turn to for additional information or help. The local poverty agencies have frequently preempted this information and referral function as their own, but there is much more to be done in fulfilling this function adequately.

For the most part libraries have not yet begun to explore the limits of feasibility and relevance in response to user needs and requirements. Most of the programs that were visited embody very familiar activities and approaches: ethnically oriented book collections, story hours, bookmobiles, movies, etc. However, the analysis of program activities suggests that in the few programs where these standard or conventional activities have been successful in attracting adults or in increasing the number of users, they have been approached by libraries in a conscious and competitive effort to market a revitalized product.

The concepts of program effectiveness or program success or failure were developed in terms of a systems approach to the program cycle of input, implementation, and output. Strategic points within the cycle were identified at which readings could be taken as to the effectiveness of the program. For programs to be optimally effective, the following criteria were suggested as the standard for evaluation:

1. Program objectives should be related to individual and community needs, i.e., to user requirements
2. Program planning and implementation should carry forward program objectives
3. Program output should reflect the achievement of program objectives and hence the satisfaction of user needs and requirements
4. Program inputs (costs) should be appropriate to the level of program output.

The study findings have been shaped by the underlying premise that in setting program objectives libraries should adopt the prevailing social view of education. This view holds that education and educationally related efforts, particularly for low-income groups, should function as a vehicle for social and economic mobility. The interview data confirm that this view is in fact held by the disadvantaged, and that the public library is valued by both groups and individuals primarily in terms of its usefulness in promoting this mobility. To meet the needs of the disadvantaged, it becomes the responsibility of social institutions to move as far as is feasible and appropriate to rectify the existing inequality of opportunity for human growth and development.

Given these objectives, or at least a general commitment to meet community needs, and given a general lack of innovation in project activity or program strategy, the most important determinants of program success or failure appear at this stage to be factors of program implementation.

Although the cities visited represented a diverse assortment of city sizes, program types, and groups served, certain fundamental program elements recurred in city after city as highly correlated with program success or failure. These basic program factors critical to program effectiveness include the following:

1. Competency and effectiveness of staff
2. Degree of community involvement and understanding of community dynamics evidenced by project
3. Degree of autonomy exercised by project director in decision making
4. Quality of materials used
5. Effectiveness of publicity, or project visibility.

In general, the exigencies of low-income urban society seem to require that all of these elements be positive to a high degree; the absence of one or more is not merely a program deficiency but appears to lead more or less rapidly to program failure.

The major deficiency in the data and information available to the study was the lack of any detailed knowledge of the impact of the programs upon the intended target group. Existing procedures for or interest in measurement of program outputs were generally found to be fragmentary and inadequate. This was not necessarily owing to methodological or measurement difficulties; most programs have as an explicit or implicit objective increasing the number of library users, yet few libraries actually count users. On the basis of the field observations, it appears that the number of library users or participants in most library-sponsored activities in ghetto areas is small in relation to the size of the target group it is desired to reach. In many cases the numbers are particularly unsatisfactory when viewed in conjunction with the costs of the program.

The study findings point to three major policy recommendations for achieving greater effectiveness and impact of public library service to the disadvantaged:

1. The implementation of existing programs must be improved and strengthened
2. Libraries must augment their ability to plan and program effectively through greater use of systems approaches and improved data collection
3. New roles must be explored for the public library as a resource for experience, opportunities, and stimuli not readily available elsewhere.

Most of this book has been devoted to an analysis of existing programs and to an assessment of strengths and weaknesses in current program activities. The critical importance of staff competency, community involvement, program autonomy, and other specific aspects of program implementation has been spelled out.

Also libraries must acquire a better grasp of how existing programs and activities can be more directly oriented to meet expressed needs and priorities. The need for better data collection is imperative. It is related, however, to the need for a general systems approach to planning and operating library programs, which is the second major policy recommendation. The effectiveness of the public library in delivering services to the public requires the orientation of library administrators to a program-planning and budgeting approach, and to an understanding of the necessary skills, which include not only professional library skills but also professional planning, leadership, and management. In the longer term most public libraries will doubtless be required to adopt some form of program budgeting as it gains widespread acceptance at the municipal government level. Familiarity with the basic approach should convince libraries of the importance of program budgeting as a planning tool (and as a technique helpful in commanding public support for library expenditures in general), and also of the importance of having available an adequate data base as a foundation for decision making.

Specifically, there are three types of data that libraries could collect fairly easily, more or less as they were collected for this study:

1. Systematic observation and analysis of program outreach and impact
2. Community needs and resources
3. Felt needs of users and potential users.

There are a variety of ways in which data can be collected: from existing documents, by interview, observation, questionnaire, management reporting forms, etc. Determination by individual libraries of which sources or techniques should be used must include considerations of cost, convenience and ease of collection, reliability of data, and possible disruption to ongoing operations. In many cases no one procedure can satisfy all of these considerations, and some priorities must be established; however, the quality of data collection and range of effectiveness measures can be substantially improved over present levels at relatively little cost by collecting and analyzing information readily available.

In most of the cities visited, the base unit for whatever information is collected concerning library users, participants in activities, circulation, and other detailed data is the monthly report by the branch. Special projects or programs are frequently not even required to report monthly but on a quarterly, semiannual, or annual basis. These annual program or project reports are frequently subjective, narrative accounts of highlights of the previous year and optimistic hopes for the one ahead. Monthly statistical branch reports, as noted earlier, are mainly concerned with circulation and accessions.

A first and simple step, then, would be to count, on a total or sample basis, the number of branch or program users. A next step would attempt to find out something about the characteristics and interests of patrons. None of the libraries studied, for example, keep the kind of detailed daily records maintained by a new inner-city library under the sponsorship of the Queens Borough (New

144 Conclusions and Recommendations

York) Public Library. That center collects the following information on a *daily* basis:

Circulation
Analysis of adult materials circulated (subject or kind)
Number of patrons
Type of programs or activities and number of participants by age group
Weather and/or other special conditions
Number of persons given information
Specific types of information given
Specific requests for books, records, or information not available
Number of persons listening to records or tapes
Titles of records used
Number and age group of children being tutored or helped with homework
Specific materials needed for homework and not available
Anecdotal record noting any increased interest or participation by individuals or groups, or anything else of interest.

The Queens plan in this new center, as in other projects for the disadvantaged which they have sponsored, is to collect this information daily for an initial period and then reduce the reporting frequency to a weekly basis when the program administrator feels that weekly feedback will be adequate. The specific items of information collected are directly related to strengthening and improving the program by recording what is needed, as well as what is preferred. This type of information tells the library what kinds of people are using its services, which services and materials are more effective and which less so, as well as providing simple counts of library use.

Additional information on program functioning at individual branches or projects might feasibly be collected as it has been in this study, i.e., through structured interview, observation, and report by a designated agent, preferably not a regular employee of the library staff. This type of information can be collected at regular intervals, perhaps annually, or as required to support program policy and long-range budgeting.

Feedback from other community institutions can most usefully be acquired by those library staff members, such as branch librarians, project directors, and outreach workers, who regularly have contact with these institutions.

A number of libraries currently record the fact of contact, i.e., talks to outside groups, activities held in the library, etc., but without the kind of additional information that would facilitate analysis for planning and evaluation purposes.

Libraries should also consider data collection to gather information concerning nonuser residents in their service areas. In the course of the field visits, it was apparent that the residents of urban ghettos, particularly in the larger cities, are frequently surveyed by various public and private groups. (In fact, resentment was expressed in two or three cities at "all the surveys and no action.") Libraries could participate with other groups at the outset of the survey planning to collect whatever particular information they need, if they do not wish to conduct a survey of their own. The purpose of such surveys should be to focus upon what is unique about the neighborhood or community, its specific problems and interests, and ways in which the library might be perceived as increasingly useful, as well as the community assessment of the value of the library's services.

None of these various data collection techniques, however, can collect the kind of program impact information that would be furnished by a classic experimental design. If a library program is designed to make a fairly substantial impact upon a predetermined group of individuals, it should be possible to build some sort of pre- and post-measures, or possibly even some experimental/control group comparisons, into the program. Longitudinal follow-up studies of children or young adults who have participated in a sustained library activity should be undertaken.

There is an obvious and valuable pool of subjects for this type of study in current child users, since casual observation suggests, and the user data confirm, that most of them come to the library more frequently than once a week, and many every day. The amount of exposure to library influence for these children, if measured only in terms of hours per week, is therefore potentially large enough to make it worthwhile to investigate their subsequent development. It may well be that it is difficult to isolate self-selection factors operating in these subjects from library program impact, but such studies should at least indicate whether or not frequent library use is a reliable predictor of future educational or other achievement by disadvantaged children.

Program cost data is another area in which substantially improved reporting would assist library systems in monitoring their own efforts as well as facilitating cost-effectiveness comparisons between programs. There are several difficulties with existing cost data. The first, and by far the most important, is that relatively few libraries utilize a program budgeting system. Adequate program cost data are available primarily from projects which have been funded in their entirety by federal sources and for which program sponsors were obliged to prepare a budget as part of the proposal. Otherwise the cost picture is blurred, even in projects where federal funds form part of the total cost.

Regardless of funding sources, the services or programs for the disadvantaged are not always a distinct entity, in fact or in the minds of the library fiscal officers, which presents many problems in allocating costs. There are also difficulties in allocating costs when a library department (such as processing or public relations) performs some partial services for a program serving the disadvantaged. Finally, there are additional problems in securing compatibility of cost data which are caused by different fiscal year bases for different funding sources, inadequate identification of various budget revisions, incomplete or delayed reporting of actual expenditures, differing accounting methods of reporting certain categories of expenditure (e.g., processing and fringe benefits), and similar technical questions.

If these kinds of data were collected by libraries, the information would be directly useful in advancing what is known at both federal and local levels about programming. It should be possible to look at program functions, including objectives, planning, and implementation, and select what appear to be replicable, controllable program features associated with program success. These features can then be applied to a subsequent group of sample programs, thus providing successive opportunities to isolate and evaluate results. Within a branch or single program, such information is equally useful as the basis for improving, modifying, or expanding the program.

The third major policy recommendation concerns the possibility of meeting current needs, and anticipating those of the future, in new ways—i.e., through programs or activities which individuals in low-income communities may not have experienced and therefore not considered or expected from the public library. This area of unfelt needs includes the possibilities that technological advance and education innovation are now opening up to view, such as closed-circuit television, computer terminals, and simulation games. In a sense the library does not depart from one of its traditional functions as keeper of scarce resources. It merely recognizes that for knowledge and communication, books are no longer the monopoly resource. Not only hardware but also sensory and environmental stimuli are the scarce resources, at least in low-income areas, and libraries should seriously consider the possibilities of joining with other educational and cultural institutions, such as zoos, parks, and museums, to present a creative, stimulating approach to learning as a part of the human experience. We have already seen that successful programs seem to require large amounts of dollar resources; certainly one way to assemble resources which may be beyond the budget of a single agency is through the joint participation of several institutions.

The balance of this chapter sketches out some of these new directions for public library services in the fields of education, information, recreation, and culture.

Education. The need for more effective integration of public libraries with schools at all levels is strong and clear. All segments of the community are concerned with formal education as a human and political priority, since a major channel for upward mobility of the poor lies in the acquisition of cognitive skills and educational credentials.

Current users of inner-city libraries are almost entirely children and others enrolled in formal educational programs. If library resources in ghetto areas were more closely coordinated with school resources, there might be enough financial support to provide for many services and much equipment that neither can now afford. In one city a government official expressed the idea that for maximum operating efficiency there should be a single library system operating public libraries in schools and elsewhere. There are many respondents who want to see closer ties between school and library during school hours, i.e., greater utilization of public libraries as part of the ongoing curriculum. Poverty agencies are particularly interested in more of what they already see as related to formal educational achievement—tutoring, remedial reading, and preschool programs. Presumably they would support any type of joint projects aimed at improving educational achievement.

From a financial point of view, a more integrated approach to planning would be both feasible and beneficial. Annual expenditures for the majority of special library programs or ghetto branches studied range from about $50,000 to $100,000 per year. In a given library service area there may easily be ten to twenty public and private schools, each spending from $1000 to $5000 per year for library materials. With this much money and some long-range planning, it would be possible to put into almost any ghetto area a library facility as comprehensive and lavish as might be desired. It could include, for example, special programs and other curriculum supplements prepared or recorded by teachers and stored on tape, including interviews and discussions with famous artists, writers, and high government officials. It could be designed to include amenities such as an enormous fireplace to sit and read in front of on cold winter afternoons.

The idea of establishing public libraries as contributors to the learning environment of the schools is an integral part of much contemporary planning for new educational/cultural centers, educational parks, and similar innovative educational facilities. It can certainly be tried out in the roomy old buildings now located in ghetto areas, since it depends at least as much on joint planning and working relations as it does on infusion of new or additional resources. These ghetto branches could join with zoos, parks, and museums, as noted above, to offer combinations of field trips, visual presentations, and reference materials that would present learning as a part of the human experience, a creative sensory approach backed up by independent study or self-starting reading projects at any level.

Improved coordination of library resources with those of public schools should have a direct and immediate effect upon expanding what is now the single strong market for urban library services in disadvantaged areas, the student. In some low-income branches visited, as noted in chapter 2, up to 95 percent of library users are aged eighteen and under. If these branches were utilized as special school-oriented resource centers and their offerings expanded and enriched, they should attract a significant percentage of the student population.

There are also new possibilities for educational activity directed to adults. Libraries would be responsive to community needs if they included training for those already holding leadership potential in low-income communities. Several poverty agencies, for example, expressed an interest in subjects such as organizational development, parliamentary procedures, and topics of political or sociological interest. Generally library concern with adult education in low-income areas is focused on basic literacy needs and related concerns; it might also be profitable to consider the possibilities of meeting more sophisticated needs for technical assistance to community groups. Such activities would make the library useful to "important people," and set up an example that less important people might wish to emulate. Equipment such as closed-circuit television, game simulation centers, news tickers, and computer terminals would establish the prestige and popularity of the library with the elite of the local community, at the same time that it offers to these adults opportunities for learning not available elsewhere.

Information. It is probable that the urban poor are now better informed than they ever were about the availability of services and assistance from the social sector. However, at least half of the library nonusers interviewed in this study are still ignorant of information sources in many areas, and libraries could usefully provide information specific to the state, city, or neighborhood concerning:

Opportunities in employment, higher education, housing, etc.
Procedures for application or admissions for various programs and securing of various social services
Legislation, including local codes, tenants' rights, etc.

Collecting and maintaining this type of information would require a considerable manpower effort, since much of the procedural type of information, for example, rests upon unwritten administrative practices which may need to be learned about individually and through personal visit. The information collected must be that which is specifically needed by individuals in that community in the conduct of their daily lives; it needs to be updated frequently and to be made available under circumstances which provide dignity and complete acceptance for the person seeking the information. Further, the information and referral role has been assumed in many cities by the Community Action Program and Model Cities agencies, which have interagency contacts, indigenous staffs, and other characteristics that make them potentially more effective in this function. However, there is clearly room for more than one source dispensing information, and libraries might consider, as one respondent suggested, making city hall the focus of their effort and learning everything that any citizen might need or wish to know, practically speaking, about dealing with city agencies or departments.

Another possible way to ensure information, and in fact a total program, that meets adult needs is to institute some measure of active community control. Several of the libraries visited had organized citizen advisory groups at one time or another, but none of these lasted very long. None had any active community control, but one of the cities visited was about to set up a demonstration branch to be completely run by a community group. This is a promising approach to stimulating adult interest and concern.

Recreation. Libraries have generally avoided the techniques that are considered standard by social organizations for attracting and retaining community interest. Libraries do not seem to sponsor covered-dish suppers, alumni dinners, annual balls, bake sales, fairs, or baseball teams. They ought to do all of these things, or at least all those that are feasible. People respond favorably to the implicit friendliness and hospitality of social occasions; they feel warmer toward an organization which offers them food and drink. The book publishing world has made a cliché of cocktail parties to introduce books and authors; receptions are held by all sorts of educational or cultural groups to promote art, opera, symphony, and ballet, yet it is rare to find libraries offering this type of social/recreational activity. The few that do have found these kinds of activities to be very useful.

Libraries ought also to consider adding food as a permanent attraction—a European-style coffee bar, an ice cream parlor, or a similar attractive facility with adequate space for leisurely snacking and talking. Naturally, recreational functions should be so located as not to interfere with patrons who are using the library for reading and study.

Culture. The cultural activities of ghetto libraries have been almost universally successful. Several of the cities visited had offered at one time or another black art, music, dance and drama,

Chicano documentaries and study prints, and live theatrical presentations of puppet shows, folk singers, and similar attractions. Two cities offered ongoing workshops in drama or photography. All of these programs and activities have attracted capacity crowds.

The lack of cultural exposure in low-income communities is substantial: 65 percent of the nonusers interviewed have never been to a concert, 79 percent have never been to a museum, and 83 percent have never been to an art exhibit. Clearly the need here is very great, and one in which libraries could successfully participate. In the cities visited, the major constraints have been those of facilities. Adequate accommodations for large audiences are difficult to find in low-income neighborhoods. Nonetheless, this is a very promising area for library participation, particularly in developing and sponsoring cultural "happenings." Cultural activities designed to reflect and develop the heritage, traditions, and history of minority groups are particularly important in meeting the objectives of urban libraries. These activities build acceptance and self-esteem through pleasurable and gratifying activities, at the same time opening new fields for growth in cognitive skills and more sophisticated perceptions.

This area of cultural enrichment is another in which urban libraries might join with museums, parks, and private organizations to provide the necessary scale of sustenance and support. Where libraries have sponsored cultural events by themselves, they have been chiefly one-time events. The impact, whether cultural or political, is then dissipated because there is no organizational follow-up or resource for developing and maintaining the community interest, and no ongoing group of professionals to offer continuing resources in the particular specialty.

In each of these areas—education, information, recreation, and culture—the need for better planning and for planning in cooperation with other institutions emerges as essential. In many instances this planning and coordination will need to take place at federal and at state levels as well as at the local level, if effective progress is to be made. Libraries may in fact find their activities severely curtailed unless the financial difficulties of program funding are faced realistically. Adequate programs require sizable budgets, while at the same time rising costs are forcing local governments to reappraise ever more closely the allocation of funds. The federal flow, or at least part of it, is also likely to be channeled through revenue sharing for allocation by state and local governments. The competing claims of a voluntary agency such as the public library will be substantially discounted unless it can demonstrate a clearly defined and measurable degree of social utility.

Appendix A: Data Collection Instruments

THE COMPLETE instrument package for the study consisted of three basic instruments, with variations of each for different groups of respondents. The three basic instruments were a program interview guide, a user-nonuser questionnaire, and a community interview guide. Nine variations of these three forms were used in this study:

Program interview guides
1. System level
2. Branch level
3. Program level
User/nonuser questionnaires
4. User questionnaire
5. Nonuser questionnaire
Community interview guides
6. School interview guide
7. Poverty agency
8. City government
9. Library board of trustees.

A typical form in each category is reproduced in this appendix. These are the branch program interview guide, the nonuser questionnaire, and the school interview guide.

154 *Appendix A*

BRANCH PROGRAM INTERVIEW GUIDE

BOB 51 S69025
Exp. 12/70

Date_____

City_____

Phone_____   LIBRARY STUDY   Branch level

Name of interviewee_____ Title_____

I. I would like to begin by asking you whether this branch is different in any way from the others?

☐Yes ☐No   If yes, how?

1. Specific Program Focus: Now I would like to know about the specific program that we are studying for the disadvantaged at your library.

2. Did the staff of this branch originate the program? ☐Yes ☐No
   If no, how did it come to you?

   ☐a. Generally within the system
   ☐b. Community organization
   ☐c. City government
   ☐d. State government
   ☐e. School board
   ☐f. Other (specify) _____

INTERVIEWER: IF IT WAS THE IDEA OF A PARTICULAR PERSON, ASK:

What position does this person hold?_____

3. What do you consider to be the specific objectives or purposes of the program (by activity)? List all that apply.

   Activity 1

   a._____

   b._____

   c._____

   d._____

   Activity 2

   a._____

   b._____

   c._____

   d._____

Activity 3

a._____

b._____

c._____

d._____

Activity 4

a._____

b._____

c._____

d._____

4. If more than one objective named, which do you view as the <u>most</u> important purpose of each activity?

Activity

1._____

2._____

3._____

4._____

5. Would you like to see a change in the objectives for any of the activities?

☐Yes ☐No

If yes, which activities and what should the objectives be?

1._____

2._____

3._____

4._____

II. Other Programs for the Disadvantaged. Now we'd like to know a few things about the other programs the branch sponsors, if any.

6. Are there any other specific programs for the disadvantaged operating at or through this branch? ☐Yes   ☐No
If yes, what are they?

	Program		
	1	2	3
TITLE OF PROGRAM			
a. Activity			
b. Emphasis (distribution of materials or outreach)			
c. Target group. . .			
d. Materials and equipment			
e. Facilities			
f. Scheduling			
g. Personnel assigned to activity and duties.			

7. In general, what changes in these programs have taken place in the last 4 years?

Activities:

Target group:

Materials and equipment:

Facilities:

Scheduling:

Emphasis (distribution of materials or
   outreach):

8. What do you consider to be the objectives of each of your programs?

Program 1

a._____

b._____

c._____

d._____

Program 2

a._____

b._____

c._____

d._____

Program 3

a._____

b._____

c._____

d._____

Program 4

a._____

b._____

c._____

d._____

9. If more than one objective named, which do you view as the <u>most</u> important purpose of each program?

   Program

   1._____

   2._____

   3._____

   4._____

10. Have any recommendations for program change, additions, etc. been made by you and not approved?   ☐Yes ☐No

    If yes, what were these recommendations?_____

    _____

    _____

    At what level were they turned down?

       ☐1. Local library hierarchy
       ☐2. Local government hierarchy
       ☐3. State government
       ☐4. Federal government

III. Routine Branch Operation

Books and nonbook materials. (Note: Get detailed description only if program has no collection of its own or if program collection is the branch collection. Otherwise, just a general description of the collection.)

11. We'd like to have an idea of the composition of your book collection.

Total Number of Books

Total Fiction . . . . _____

Total Nonfiction . . . . _____

    Plays and Poetry . . . . _____

    How-to Books . . . . _____

    Black History and culture . . . . _____

Generally Books by Black Authors. . . . _____

Books for Spanish Speaking Individuals _____

Easy-to-Read Books for Adults . . . . . _____

Children's Books . . . . _____

    Comics . . . . _____

Paperbacks . . . . _____

12. a. Can we have a list of magazines and newspapers currently sub-scribed to? ☐Yes ☐No

   b. Have any changes taken place in the list of periodicals you subscribe to over the last 4 years? ☐Yes ☐No

   c. If yes, what are these changes? _____

13. Please tell me the number of records and tapes of various kinds that comprise your collection. Total number

    Classical. . . . . _____

    Popular. . . . . _____

       Rock/Soul/Other folk, ethnic. . . _____

    Children's . . . . _____

    Language learning· . . . . _____

    Readings of plays/poetry . . . . _____

    Other (specify) . . . . _____

    TOTAL RECORDS AND TAPES · · · · · · · _____

14. Do you have any other types of materials in or available through the library other than books, periodicals, or records/tapes? ☐Yes ☐No
If yes, please describe these other materials. _____

15. Do you lend books to or put library/classroom collections in the schools? ☐Yes ☐No

16. Please provide the following information concerning your staff:	Number paid and having:					
	Library Science degrees			Other college degrees	No College Degree	Number of volunteers
	4th yr B.L.S.	5th yr B.L.S.	M.L.S.			
Total						
Age:						
under 21	___	___	___	___	___	___
21-25.	___	___	___	___	___	___
26-40.	___	___	___	___	___	___
41-60.	___	___	___	___	___	___
over 60.	___	___	___	___	___	___
Sex:						
male	___	___	___	___	___	___
female	___	___	___	___	___	___
Race or ethnic origin:						
(minority group members only--total number)						
Negro.	___	___	___	___	___	___
Oriental	___	___	___	___	___	___
American Indian. . . .	___	___	___	___	___	___
Spanish surname. . . .	___	___	___	___	___	___
Other (specify). . . .	___	___	___	___	___	___
Residence:						
Live in lib svce area	___	___	___	___	___	___
Live in commun. with similar socio-econ. characteristics . . .	___	___	___	___	___	___
Live in commun. with different character- istics.	___	___	___	___	___	___
Work experience						
Library.	___	___	___	___	___	___
Work with disadvan- taged--Vista, Peace Corps, etc.	___	___	___	___	___	___
Other	___	___	___	___	___	___
Teaching	___	___	___	___	___	___
None	___	___	___	___	___	___
Other.	___	___	___	___	___	___
Special skills	___	___	___	___	___	___
Special insvce training	___	___	___	___	___	___
Special pre-svce train'g	___	___	___	___	___	___

Impact Measures

17. Do you have any way of estimating the effectiveness of your program?
    ☐Yes ☐No

    If yes, what do you use?_____

    _____

    _____

18. Do you keep any of the following types of data?   Yes No

    a. Circulation count . . . . ☐ ☐

    b. Number coming into branch or other facility , ... ☐ ☐

    c. Number participating in activity. . . . . ☐ ☐

    d. Occupancy count . . . . ☐ ☐

    e. Other type of head count (specify). . . . . ☐ ☐
       _____

    f. Number of new titles. . . . . ☐ ☐

    g. Number of library cards issued . . . . ☐ ☐

    h. Amount of new equipment . . . . ☐ ☐

    i. Request for services. . . . . ☐ ☐

    j. Reactions from individuals, agencies, newspapers, etc. . . . ☐ ☐

    k. Increased involvement with other agencies . . . . ☐ ☐

    l. Follow-up on individual participants . . . . ☐ ☐

    m. Gifts, fund raising effort from community . . . . ☐ ☐

    n. Other (specify)_____ . . . . . . ☐ ☐

19a. What data can you provide on the measures you have taken? (Get copies of anything—reports, etc.—rather than write everything down)

    Measure   Data

    _____   _____

    _____   _____

  b. What type of program reporting forms do you use? (Describe and get samples.)

    _____

20. Do you have any new ideas for impact measures that you might use if you had more money and time?
    ☐Yes ☐No

    If yes, specify _____

    _____

162 *Appendix A*

Decision Making

21. Who is responsible for
decisions in the follow-
ing areas?

	A	B	C	D	E	F	G	H	I	J	K
a. Which groups will be served by the project .											
b. What program shall consist of.											
c. What materials and equipment will be used											
d. What facilities will be used											
e. Who is to be hired as staff member members (different levels). . .											

Code: A. Project director
B. Local library system
C. State library system
D. Federal government
E. Branch head

F. Community organizations
G. School system
H. Library advisory board
I. Board of trustees
J. Local city government

K. Other (specify)_____

Descriptions of Target Population

22. Since your target population is actually all the people who live in this
area, we'd like you to know how you would characterize this population.

Race and Ethnic Origin: Nonminority group members . . _____%

Negro . . . . _____

Oriental . . . . _____

American Indian . . . . _____

Spanish surname . . . . _____

Other (specify) . . . . _____

Occupational Level: Professional, managerial . . . _____%

Other white-collar job . . . . _____

Blue-collar skilled . . . . . _____

Semi-skilled . . . . _____

Unskilled . . . . _____

Unemployed, welfare . . . . . _____

23. a. Here is a list. From those items mentioned on the list, what do you
feel are the three major needs in the area of educational/cultural/
informational services of the people living in this neighborhood?
(Code under A all responses)

 b. Of all those on the list, which do you think public libraries could
effectively serve? (Code under B)

Educational/Cultural/Informational Services	A	B
Direct Educational Services		
Tutoring	_____	_____
Remedial reading/literacy	_____	_____
After-school study center	_____	_____
Preschool programs	_____	_____
Adult education	_____	_____
Provision of educational materials to other agencies (Individual schools, training programs, etc.)		
Books and other printed materials	_____	_____
Audiovisual materials	_____	_____
Programmed learning materials	_____	_____
Educational resources for self-education		
Books and nonbook materials	_____	_____
Easy-to-read materials, self-learning texts, etc.	_____	_____
Community information and referral service		
Community center for meetings, etc.	_____	_____
Cultural enrichment		
Music, dance, theater, art, photography . . .	_____	_____
Motivating agency—to encourage		
Interest in learning	_____	_____
Parental support for children's educational development	_____	_____
Communication between various groups in the community.	_____	_____

Outside Involvement and Interaction beyond or in addition to normal working
or organizational relations with other levels or agencies.

24. For each of the following groups, please state the type of involvement
each has with the program and the extent of this involvement.

	Code	Describe involvement
a. Local federally funded programs (specify) OEO, Labor Department, Model City programs, etc.	_____	_____
b. State government	_____	_____
c. Local government (Get point of contact)	_____	_____
d. Other neighborhood community groups (name)	_____	_____
e. Schools (indicate type and level).	_____	_____
f. Other (specify)	_____	_____

Code: A. None
       B. Set objective   E. Funding
       C. Program planning   F. Advisory
       D. Operating   G. Other (specify)
          D1. Materials and equipment   _____
          D2. Facilities
          D3. Personnel

25. Of those you've named above, which one do you think has had the most
influence on the branch? _____

Why?_____

26. Does the branch staff have meetings? ☐Yes ☐No

If yes, how often?_____

27. Does the branch library have joint meetings for project staff and regular
library personnel? ☐Yes ☐No

If yes, how often?_____

28. What is the degree of independence between project and regular library
staff?
    ☐Very independent   ☐Somewhat independent
    ☐Somewhat dependent   ☐Very dependent

29. Describe the relationship between the project and regular library staff:
    ☐Excellent ☐Good ☐Fair ☐Poor

30. To whom do you as a branch head report? _____
    ☐ System level ☐ Other (specify)_____

What is the administrative relationship between you and the project head?

_____

31. What methods do you use to inform community of your programs? How effective do you think they are?

	How effective
circulars/posters/flyers	
radio/TV/papers--paid	
radio/TV/papers--news items	
public schools	
community organizations	
outreach workers	
word of mouth	
other?	

What improvements, if any, would you like to be made?

_____

_____

Overview

32. And finally, what do you consider to be the role of the library in the community? _____

      a. provide books and nonbook materials; traditional reference source
      b. provide direct educational services--tutoring, adult education, place to study, etc.
      c. provide resources for continuing (self) education
      d. place of social interaction
      e. community information center
      f. fulfill cultural needs
      g. concerned helping agency/outreach
      h. other (specify)_____

33. Do you think that any of the special services, programs, or activities should be retained as part of the regular library services?

    ☐Yes ☐No

If yes, which ones?_____

For what reasons? _____

N O N U S E R   Q U E S T I O N N A I R E

BOB 51 S69025
Exp. 12/70

No. _____   NU   10-1

Interviewer _____   Interview Site _____

Date _____   City _____   FU   10-2

Hello, I wonder if I could talk to you for a few minutes? I'm working for Behavior Science Corporation   UH   10-3
and we'd like to find out   how people get information about community services. Could I ask you a
few questions?

HAND CARD TO RESPONDENT – BE SURE
TO READ LOCAL NAME ON CARD

On this card are different types of programs
and services available to people in this area.
I'd like to ask you about them.

1. Have you ever heard of the Community
   Action Agency, _____?

   Yes   11-1 [ ]
   No   11-2 [ ]

   IF YES:

   How do you know about the Community
   Action Agency? (CHECK ONE)

   Have been there, used service, visited   12-1 [ ]
   Friends, neighbors, relatives, or family   12-2 [ ]
   Radio, television, newspaper   12-3 [ ]
   Other(specify) _____   12-4 [ ]

   When was the last time you used the
   Community Action Agency?

   Within the last week   13-1 [ ]
   Within last month   13-2 [ ]
   Within last 6 months   13-3 [ ]
   Over 6 months ago   13-4 [ ]
   Never/don't know   13-5 [ ]

2. Have you ever heard of the Pre-School
   Program, _____?

   Yes   14-1 [ ]
   No   14-2 [ ]

IF YES:

How do you know about the Pre-School
Program? (CHECK ONE)

Have been there, used service, visited   15-1 [ ]
Friends, neighbors, relatives, or family   15-2 [ ]
Radio, television, newspaper   15-3 [ ]
Other(specify) _____   15-4 [ ]

When was the last time you used the
Pre-School Program?

Within last week   16-1 [ ]
Within last month   16-2 [ ]
Within last 6 months   16-3 [ ]
Over 6 months ago   16-4 [ ]
Never/don't know   16-5 [ ]

3. Have you ever heard of the Adult
   Education Program, _____?

   Yes   17-1 [ ]
   No   17-2 [ ]

IF YES:

How do you know about the Adult
Education Program? (CHECK ONE)

Have been there, used it, visited   18-1 [ ]
Friends, neighbors,relatives, or family   18-2 [ ]
Radio,television, newspaper   18-3 [ ]
Other(specify) _____   18-4 [ ]

When was the last time you used the Adult
Education Program?

Within the last week   19-1 [ ]
Within last month   19-2 [ ]
Within last 6 months   19-3 [ ]
Over 6 months ago   19-4 [ ]
Never/don't know   19-5 [ ]

4. Have you ever heard of the Job
   Information Center, _____?

   Yes   20-1 [ ]
   No   20-2 [ ]

IF YES:

How do you know about the Job Information Center? (CHECK ONE)

Have been there, used service, visited   21-1 [ ]
Friends, neighbors, relatives, or family   21-2 [ ]
Radio, television, newspaper   21-3 [ ]
Other(specify) _____   21-4 [ ]

When was the last time you used the
Job Information Center?

Within the last week   22-1 [ ]
Within last month   22-2 [ ]
Within last 6 months   22-3 [ ]
Over 6 months ago   22-4 [ ]
Never/don't know   22-5 [ ]

5. Have you ever heard of the Public Library,
   _____ ?

   Yes   23-1 [ ]
   No   23-2 [ ]

IF YES:

How do you know about the _____
library? (CHECK ONE)

Have been there, used service, visited   24-1 [ ]
Friends, neighbors, relatives, or family   24-2 [ ]
Radio, television, newspaper   24-3 [ ]
Other (specify) _____   24-4 [ ]

When was the last time you visited the
_____ library?

Within the last week   25-1 [ ]
Within last month   25-2 [ ]
Within last 6 months   25-3 [ ]
Over 6 months ago   25-4 [ ]
Never/don't know   25-5 [ ]

6. When you have a few hours of spare time,
   how do you most enjoy spending it?
   (CHECK ONE OR TWO)   26 - 27

   Reading   -1 [ ]
   Talking to friends   -2 [ ]
   Watching television   -3 [ ]
   Listening to records or radio   -4 [ ]
   With my family, children   -5 [ ]
   Sewing, fixing things around the house   -6 [ ]
   Sports, athletics   -7 [ ]
   Go out somewhere   -8 [ ]
   Other (specify) _____   -9 [ ]

7. During the past year have you been to a
   museum?

   Yes   28-1 [ ]
   No   28-2 [ ]

8. During the past year have you been to
   hear a concert or other live musical
   program?

   Yes   29-1 [ ]
   No   29-2 [ ]

9. During the past year have you been to an
   art exhibit?

   Yes   30-1 [ ]
   No   30-2 [ ]

10. Do you usually read the newspapers?

    Yes   31-1 [ ]
    No   31-2 [ ]

IF YES:

Which papers do you usually read?

_____
_____
_____

11. Which do you like to read, magazines or books?

Magazines	32-1 [ ]
Books	32-2 [ ]
Both	32-3 [ ]
Neither	32-4 [ ]
Don't know	32-5 [ ]

IF MAGAZINES OR BOTH IS ANSWERED:

Which magazines do you usually read?

_____

_____

_____

IF BOOKS OR BOTH IS ANSWERED:

What type of books do you usually read? (CHECK ONE)

Black history, culture	33-1 [ ]
Spanish history, culture	33-2 [ ]
Humor	33-3 [ ]
Love/adventure	33-4 [ ]
Mystery/detective stories	33-5 [ ]
School-related or reference books	33-6 [ ]
Bible	33-7 [ ]
Other (specify) _____	33-8 [ ]

12. Last week, did you watch any TV?

Yes	34-1 [ ]
No	34-2 [ ]

IF YES:

How many days of the week did you watch TV?

Every day	35-1 [ ]
Weekend only	35-2 [ ]
1 to 2 days (any others except Saturday and Sunday)	35-3 [ ]
3 to 4 days	35-4 [ ]
5 to 6 days	35-5 [ ]

13. Did you listen to the radio last week?

Yes	36-1 [ ]
No	36-2 [ ]

14. Did you do any reading last week?

Yes	37-1 [ ]
No	37-2 [ ]

IF YES:

What did you read? (CHECK ALL THAT APPLY)   38 - 41

Books	-1 [ ]
Magazines	-2 [ ]
Newspapers	-3 [ ]
Other (specify)	-4 [ ]

_____

15. Now I will read you some subjects that people often want to find out more about. Stop me when I come to the ones that would interest you or your family. (CHECK ALL THAT ARE OF INTEREST)   42 - 51

Child care	-1 [ ]
Household repairs	-2 [ ]
Medical information or help	-3 [ ]
Legal help	-4 [ ]
Birth control	-5 [ ]
Job information	-6 [ ]
Racial discrimination	-7 [ ]
Black/Spanish culture	-8 [ ]
Sports	-9 [ ]
Information on money matters	-0 [ ]

Are there any other subjects you are interested in? _____

_____

(BE SURE TO GET AS MANY AS YOU CAN)

16. Now I will read the list again. After I read each one, please tell me if you know where you could get information on that subject.

Child Care

Yes	52-1 [ ]
No	52-2 [ ]

IF YES: Where? _____

Household repairs

Yes	53-1 [ ]
No	53-2 [ ]

IF YES: Where?_____

Medical information or help

Yes	54-1 [ ]
No	54-2 [ ]

IF YES: Where? _____

Legal help

Yes	55-1 [ ]
No	55-2 [ ]

IF YES: Where? _____

Birth control

Yes	56-1 [ ]
No	56-2 [ ]

IF YES: Where? _____

Job information

Yes	57-1 [ ]
No	57-2 [ ]

IF YES: Where? _____

Racial discrimination

Yes	58-1 [ ]
No	58-2 [ ]

IF YES: Where? _____

Black/Spanish culture

Yes	59-1 [ ]
No	59-2 [ ]

IF YES: Where? _____

Sports

Yes	60-1 [ ]
No	60-2 [ ]

IF YES: Where? _____

Information on money matters

Yes	61-1 [ ]
No	61-2 [ ]

IF YES: Where? _____

17. Now I will read a few statements that describe some people's feelings about the public library. After I read each statement, please tell me whether you agree or disagree with it.

Most people don't go to the library because nothing's happening there.

Agree	62-1 [ ]
Disagree	62-2 [ ]
Don't know	63-3 [ ]

It's only for people who like to work or study.

Agree	63-1 [ ]
Disagree	63-2 [ ]
Don't know	63-3 [ ]

The library's a community organization which tries to make life more pleasant for the people in our neighborhood.

Agree	64-1 [ ]
Disagree	64-2 [ ]
Don't know	64-3 [ ]

It's mostly for people in school, especially kids.

Agree	65-1 [ ]
Disagree	65-2 [ ]
Don't know	65-3 [ ]

If you've never been inside the building it's probably easy to get lost.

Agree	66-1 [ ]
Disagree	66-2 [ ]
Don't know	66-3 [ ]

At the library you can find out what to
do or where to go if you have a problem.

Agree	67-1 [ ]	
Disagree	67-2 [ ]	
Don't know	67-3 [ ]	

The people who work in the library
understand books better than they
understand people.

Agree	68-1 [ ]	
Disagree	68-2 [ ]	
Don't know	68-3 [ ]	

It's only for people who can read well.

Agree	69-1 [ ]	
Disagree	69-2 [ ]	
Don't know	69-3 [ ]	

The library is really a place for people
who have a lot of free time, not for
people who work.

Agree	70-1 [ ]	
Disagree	70-2 [ ]	
Don't know	70-3 [ ]	

It has programs to help people.

Agree	71-1 [ ]	
Disagree	71-2 [ ]	
Don't know	71-3 [ ]	

18. Do you know what kinds of things the
public library has in it?

Yes	72-1 [ ]	
No	72-2 [ ]	

IF YES:

What are these things? (CHECK ALL THAT
APPLY)   73-77

Books	-1 [ ]
Magazines and newspapers	-2 [ ]
Records and tapes	-3 [ ]
Copying machine	-4 [ ]
Other (specify) _____	-5 [ ]

19. Do you know what kinds of services and
activities the public library has?

Yes	78-1 [ ]	
No	78-2 [ ]	

IF YES:

What are they? (CHECK ALL THAT   11 - 15
APPLY)

Tutoring	-1 [ ]
Children's programs	-2 [ ]
Adult education	-3 [ ]
Dances, movies, music	-4 [ ]
Other (specify) _____	-5 [ ]

HAND CARD TO RESPONDENT

20. Now I will read you a list of materials
and activities the public library does have
or could have. Stop me when I come to
something that interests you.(CHECK ALL
THAT INTEREST RESPONDENT)   16 - 24

Books, magazines, or newspapers	-1 [ ]
Movies, records, and tapes	-2 [ ]
Art exhibits/pictures	-3 [ ]
Bookmobile	-4 [ ]
Copying machine	-5 [ ]
Children's programs	-6 [ ]
Adult education, reading program	-7 [ ]
Free entertainment like movies, dances, music	-8 [ ]
Information on job training and other community services	-9 [ ]

YOU MAY READ THE LIST A SECOND
TIME

I would like some general information about you and your family so we can learn about the needs of persons of different ages and interests.

HAND CARD TO RESPONDENT

21. Here is a card with age groups. Which letter indicates your age group?

a.	Under 8	25-1 [ ]
b.	8 to 9	25-2 [ ]
c.	10 to 11	25-3 [ ]
d.	12 to 15	25-4 [ ]
e.	16 to 18	25-5 [ ]
f.	19 to 25	25-6 [ ]
g.	26 to 40	25-7 [ ]
h.	41 to 60	25-8 [ ]
i.	Over 60	25-9 [ ]

22. What was the last grade of school you completed?

1st thru 3rd grade	26-1 [ ]
4th to 6th grade	26-2 [ ]
7th to 8th grade	26-3 [ ]
9th to 11th grade	26-4 [ ]
Finished high school	26-5 [ ]
Some college or technical	26-6 [ ]
Finished college	26-7 [ ]
Graduate study	26-8 [ ]

23. Are you now attending regular school?

Yes	27-1 [ ]
No	27-2 [ ]

Are you now in any kind of educational or vocational training program?

Yes	28-1 [ ]
No	28-2 [ ]

IF YES:

What kind of program are you in?

_____

_____

What agency provides it?

_____

Where does the program meet?

_____

24. How many people in your family are living at home?

1-3	29-1 [ ]
4-6	29-2 [ ]
7-9	29-3 [ ]
over 9	29-4 [ ]

25. Did you mention earlier that you had visited the _____ library in the past?

Yes	30-1 [ ]
No	30-2 [ ]

IF NO, SKIP TO QUESTION #37

IF YES, ASK:

26. Did you say you have been at the library within the last six months?

Yes	31-1 [ ]
No	31-2 [ ]

IF NO, SKIP TO QUESTION #35

IF YES, ASK:

27. How do you usually get to the library?

Walk	32-1 [ ]
Bus	32-2 [ ]
Drive car	32-3 [ ]
Get a ride in car	32-4 [ ]
Bike	32-5 [ ]
Other _____	32-6 [ ]

28. How many blocks is it from the library to where you live?

Less than one block	33-1 [ ]
1 to 3 blocks	33-2 [ ]
4 to 6 blocks	33-3 [ ]
7 to 9 blocks	33-4 [ ]
10 to 12 blocks	33-5 [ ]
13 blocks or over	33-6 [ ]

29. How often do you go to the library?

Once a week or more	34-1 [ ]
Once a month or more	34-2 [ ]
Once in six months or more	34-3 [ ]
Less than once in six months	34-4 [ ]

30. When did you start coming to the _____ library?

This year	35-1 [ ]
Last year	35-2 [ ]
Within the last 4 years	35-3 [ ]
Over 4 years ago	35-4 [ ]

31. Did you use another library before this one?

	Yes	36-1 [ ]
	No	36-2 [ ]

32. Do you have a library card?

	Yes	37-1 [ ]
	No	37-2 [ ]

IF YES:

When did you get it?

This year	38-1 [ ]
Last year	38-2 [ ]
Within the last 4 years	38-3 [ ]
Over 4 years ago	38-4 [ ]

33. Why do you usually go to the library? (CHECK UP TO 3)   39-41

To participate in library program	-1 [ ]
To study or get help with school work	-2 [ ]
To get job information or books	-3 [ ]
To find out about a subject other than jobs	-4 [ ]
To get novels for enjoyment	-5 [ ]
To bring or pick up children	-6 [ ]
To be with friends	-7 [ ]
To attend meetings	-8 [ ]
To read in library	-9 [ ]
To use copying machine	-0 [ ]
Other(specify) _____	-x [ ]

IF NO PROGRAM: SKIP TO # 37

IF THERE IS A PROGRAM: ASK # 34

34. Are you or anyone in your family in the _____ program?

	Yes	42-1 [ ]
	No	42-2 [ ]

IF NO: SKIP TO #37

IF YES:

When did you or that member of your family start coming to the program?

This fall	43-1 [ ]
Before this fall	43-2 [ ]
Don't remember	43-3 [ ]

How did you first find out about the program? (CHECK ONE)

Library worker	44-1 [ ]
Friend/relative/family	44-2 [ ]
Child came first	44-3 [ ]
Walked into library or mobile unit	44-4 [ ]
Through another public agency	44-5 [ ]
Saw books in public place	44-6 [ ]
Saw or heard advertisement	44-7 [ ]
Through school	44-8 [ ]
Other(specify) _____	44-9 [ ]

What do you think is the main purpose of this program? (CHECK ONE)

To get people to use library	45-1 [ ]
To teach people to read	45-2 [ ]
To get people to read more	45-3 [ ]
To teach crafts or skill	45-4 [ ]
To help solve people's problems	45-5 [ ]
To entertain people	45-6 [ ]
To provide a place for people to get together	45-7 [ ]
Other(specify) _____	45-8 [ ]

NOW SKIP TO QUESTION # 37

35. What was your main purpose for going to the library the last time you were there? (CHECK ONE)

To participate in library program 46-1 [ ]
To study or get help with school work 46-2 [ ]
To get job information or books 46-3 [ ]
To find out about a subject other than jobs 46-4 [ ]
To get novels for enjoyment 46-5 [ ]
To bring or pick up children 46-6 [ ]
To be with friends 46-7 [ ]
To attend meetings 46-8 [ ]
To read in library 46-9 [ ]
To use copying machine 46-0 [ ]
Other (specify) _____ 46-x [ ]

36. What is the main reason you haven't returned to the library within the last six months? (CHECK ONE)

No time 47-1 [ ]
Bad hours for me 47-2 [ ]
Don't like to go out after dark 47-3 [ ]
Could never find what I wanted 47-4 [ ]
Have no need for it anymore 47-5 [ ]
Discrimination 47-6 [ ]
Other (specify) _____ 47-7 [ ]

39. In case my company needs to verify some of the data collected in this interview, can they telephone you?

Yes ( )
No ( )

IF YES:

What is your name and telephone number?

Name _____
Phone Number _____

THANK YOU

37. Are you presently employed?

Yes, full time 48-1 [ ]
Yes, part time 48-2 [ ]
No 48-3 [ ]
No, in school 48-4 [ ]
No, retired 48-5 [ ]

What type of work do you mostly do or have you done?

Building trades:carpenter, electrician, etc. 49-1 [ ]
Clerical/Sales/Office/Store 49-2 [ ]
Factory worker/mechanic 49-3 [ ]
Hotel/restaurant worker 49-4 [ ]
Janitor/maintenance/laborer 49-5 [ ]
Maid 49-6 [ ]
Nurse 49-7 [ ]
Teacher 49-8 [ ]
Nurse aide/teacher aide/community aide 49-9 [ ]
Other(specify) _____ 49-0 [ ]

HAND CARD TO RESPONDENT

38. Please look at this card and tell me which letter indicates the total weekly income received by all members of your family living at home.

a. Below $50 50-1 [ ]
b. $50 - $99 50-2 [ ]
c. $100 - 149 50-3 [ ]
d. $150 - $200 50-4 [ ]
e. Over $200 per week 50-5 [ ]
f. Don't know 50-6 [ ]

DO NOT ASK (JUST OBSERVE)

40. National minority group?

Yes 51-1 [ ]
No 51-2 [ ]

IF YES:

Negro 52-1 [ ]
Spanish-surnamed 52-2 [ ]
Oriental 52-3 [ ]
American Indian 52-4 [ ]
Other 52-5 [ ]

41. Sex

Male 53-1 [ ]
Female 53-2 [ ]

Appendix A

S C H O O L   I N T E R V I E W   G U I D E

Date_____   BOB 51 S69025
                                        Exp. 12/70   _____
City_____   Interviewer

_____   _____
Name and title, person being interviewed Name of school
                                          ☐Elem.   ☐Sec.   ☐Other

1. a. What do you think are the major socioeconomic characteristics of the
      student body?

        Race number   Socioeconomic status of student families:

          B _____ ___%   _____% professional, technical, managerial
          W _____ ___%   _____% white-collar, sales, clerical
          0 _____ ___%   _____% skilled and blue-collar
         AI _____ ___%   _____% lower working, semiskilled
         SS _____ ___%   _____% poverty, welfare
      Other _____ ___%

   b. How many students?_____ what grades?_____

      How many faculty (teachers/administrative/aides)? _____

2. How long have you been in this school?
      ☐less than 2 yrs. ☐3-5 yrs. ☐5-10 yrs. ☐ 10-25 yrs. ☐over 25

3. Do you live in the neighborhood? ☐Yes ☐No If yes, how long have
   you lived here?
      ☐less than 2 yrs. ☐3-10 yrs. ☐11-25 yrs. ☐over 25 yrs.

4. a. Does the school have a library? ☐Yes ☐No

   b. Librarian? ☐Yes ☐No If yes, ☐full time ☐part-time

IF THERE IS NOT A SCHOOL LIBRARY, GO TO QUESTION 8.

5. When do children have access to the school library? (Check all that apply)

      ☐only during school hrs. ☐slightly before school hrs.and slightly
      after ☐throughout the evening hrs. ☐weekends Open during summer?
      ☐Yes ☐No

6. How big is the school library?   Number of books_____

   Number of students can use room at same time for study, etc._____

7. What kinds of materials does the school library have?

      ☐course-related reference books and materials ☐books for pleasure
      reading (novels, sports, etc.), ☐records ☐films ☐other (specify)

8. Does the school have any special services or enrichment program for disadvantaged students ☐Yes ☐No

   If no, proceed to question 11.

9. What are the services for the disadvantaged?

      ☐tutoring ☐in school/remedial ☐after school/study ☐adult ed.
      ☐summer school ☐recreation ☐job training ☐cultural: music,
      dance, theater, art, photography ☐other_____

10. Does public library provide any material of other support for these?
    ☐Yes ☐No
    If yes, what?

11. a. Do you think that students are kept well aware of the services and
       programs of the library? Rate from ☐1. very well ☐2. adequate
       ☐3. poor ☐4. don't know about library at all

    b. (If 1, 2, or 3) What are the means used by the library to reach
       the students? ☐school paper ☐posters ☐visits by public library
       personnel ☐encouragement of teachers ☐other

    c. (If 2, 3, or 4) How do you think students could be made more aware
       of the public library? ☐school publications or posters ☐spon-
       sored social events ☐visits by public library personnel ☐keep
       teachers more informed of programs/encourage to tell students
       ☐other_____

    d. Are you or your staff kept informed of programs and materials avail-
       able at the library? ☐Yes ☐No If yes, how? ☐posters ☐pam-
       phlets or letters ☐newspaper ☐other_____

12. a. What do you feel are the major needs--in the area of educational/
       cultural/informational services--of the disadvantaged population
       living in the_____ neighborhood? (Code responses
       under Column A below)

    b. Which of the needs on the list do you think public libraries could
       effectively serve?(Code under B)

Educational/Cultural/Informational Services	A	B

Direct Educational Services

	A	B
Tutoring	☐	☐
Remedial reading/literacy	☐	☐
After school study center	☐	☐
Preschool programs	☐	☐
Adult education	☐	☐

Provision of educational materials to other agencies
(Individual schools, training programs, etc.)

	A	B
Books and other printed materials.	☐	☐
Audiovisual materials.	☐	☐
Programmed learning materials.	☐	☐

Educational resources for self-education

	A	B
Books and nonbook materials	☐	☐
Easy-to-read materials, self-learning texts, etc.. .	☐	☐

Community information and referrel service

	A	B
Community center for meetings, etc.	☐	☐

Cultural enrichment

	A	B
Music, dance, theater, art, photography	☐	☐

Motivating agency--to encourage--

	A	B
Interest in learning	☐	☐
Parental support for children's educational development	☐	☐
Communication between various groups in the community	☐	☐

13. Has the image of the public library changed at all over the last 3 years?
☐Yes ☐No
If yes, how and why?

14. Has the school ever cooperated with the library on any projects?
☐Yes ☐No
If yes, which projects? (open ended)

If yes, in what way did you cooperate?

☐determining objectives of program
☐planning the program
☐provision of materials and equipment
☐provision of facilities
☐provision of personnel
☐funds
☐advisory
☐other (specify)

15. Is the school administration actively interested in promoting cooperative action between the school and the library? ☐Yes ☐No

If no, why not?

☐feel such action/library is ineffectual
☐too expensive
☐administration too involved with other programs
☐doesn't feel there is a need
☐lack of interest by school personnel/administrators

16. Have there been any programs suggested by school and not carried out?
☐Yes ☐No
If yes, why not implemented?

17. What do you understand to be the major role of the public library as it
now operates?

☐provide books and nonbook materials; traditional reference source
☐provide direct educational services--tutoring, adult ed., place
to study, etc.
☐provide resources for continuing (self) education
☐place of social interaction
☐community information center
☐fulfill cultural needs
☐concerned helping agency/outreach
☐other (specify)

18. Would you like to see any changes in this role? ☐Yes ☐No

If yes, what?

19. Specifically are there any materials that you feel the library should
have, but does not or does not have enough? ☐Yes ☐No

☐more reference books
☐material specifically relevant to disadvantaged community
☐records/films
☐novels/pleasure reading
☐"how-to" books and materials
☐educational tests--reading tests, English-language instruction
☐other (specify)

Appendix B: User/Nonuser Data Collection and Analysis

IN THE survey of library users and nonusers, which is described and reported in chapters 1 and 2, approximately 200 residents of the selected branch neighborhoods were interviewed in each city, for a total of 3,524 interviews. Of this total, 1,177 were library users interviewed in the library, 569 were library users interviewed in their homes, and 1,778 were nonusers living within a half-mile radius of the library.

The data were collected in each city by teams of locally recruited interviewers. Advance arrangements with the local poverty program, state employment agency, and other neighborhood agencies had been made to generate the applicants. Approximately fifteen interviewers were selected in each city, trained to complete the questionnaire forms for collecting user/nonuser data, and supervised during the data collection by Planning Research Corporation. This procedure was followed in all but two cities. In one city the neighborhood poverty agency had its own experienced neighborhood survey team, and this team, trained by Planning Research Corporation, collected the data independently. In another city a commercial survey firm was used to collect data when unforeseen difficulties prevented recruitment of a local team.

The sampling plan for the neighborhood survey of nonusers focused upon collecting data systematically from persons who were not users of the library (defined operationally as individuals not having visited the library in the last six months) but who repre= sented potential users. Within the context of ghetto living patterns, this means individuals living close to the branch location. Therefore, the interviewing was concentrated within a half-mile radius of the branch, with a somewhat greater concentration in the blocks immediately adjacent to the library.

In each city the actual geographic area to be covered was somewhat different, since social, economic, physical, or psychological boundaries tend to delimit the neighborhood in which potential users are to be found. A sampling plan for collecting nonuser data was developed in each city based upon maps and observation of the area.

The sampling procedure which was chosen is a quota sampling method, which may be described as stratified sampling with a nonrandom selection of units within strata.

This method was selected as being, in the judgment of the study team, one which would produce results of adequate validity more economically than would more rigorous alternative methods. The method has a sufficiently high level of agreement with probability samples on questions of opinion and attitude to be appropriate for use in this study, considering that high precision estimates are not required from the sample.

The major stratification variable was distance in blocks from the library. Theoretically the sampling area was assumed to be a perfect square, with the library in the center. The square was then sectioned into quarters, with one-fourth of the sample, i.e., thirty interviews, to be collected in each quarter. The quotas are distributed through the quarter as follows:

Distance in Blocks from Library	Quota
1	10
2	10
3	6
4	4
	30

The distribution was varied somewhat in the field to compensate for the factors noted above and for extreme variation in density of dwelling units.

Approximately 150–175 interview locations were identified on the map in each city, allowing an estimated 20–30 percent overcoverage for individuals who, upon interview, might be found to be library users.

The general intent in this nonuser interviewing was to reach potential users, i.e., individuals who might be free and able to use the library at some time during its business hours. The bulk of household interviewing in these low-income areas was of necessity conducted during daylight hours, since most local interviewers were not willing to work after dark. Thus many people who work were not at home. There is a trade-off here, however, from the point of view of adequate coverage for the study, since it appears that many neighborhood residents themselves are fearful and do not come out after dark to patronize the library. Therefore, among neighborhood residents who are not at home during the day and are free to come to the library only in the evening, not many are likely to be potential library users. A fair number of ghetto residents apparently refuse to open their doors to anyone even during daylight, and many interviewers reported reluctance in this respect. For this and similar reasons the problem of nonresponders was not completely resolved in this study.

The user/nonuser questionnaires had been prepared in a computer-ready format. After editing and verification, the data were transferred to cards and then to tape. The item entries were arranged so that related items were grouped together, in the following order:

Socioeconomic characteristics
History of use of library facilities: frequency, duration of use, possession of card
Media preferences—reading, television, radio/records
Purpose of library use
Subject interest areas
Attitudes toward library
Knowledge and use of other community agencies
Knowledge and use of library (nonusers)
Knowledge of information sources in community
Knowledge of library materials and services.

For reasons related to contractual requirements, an initial compilation was made of 3,114 of the questionnaires, and these data, summarized in chapter 2, are presented in the original tabulation in table 1. The user data presented in table 1 divide users into three categories and display the data for each category

Table 1. Summary of User/Nonuser Questionnaires—OE Urban Library Study

	User/CH 465 #	%	User 712 #	%	User/H 159 #	%	Non/Former 1778 #	%
Here is a card with age groups. Which letter indicates your age group?								
a. Under 8	6	1	1	0	0	0	1	0
b. 8 to 9	96	21	3	0	0	0	3	0
c. 10 to 11	234	50	1	0	0	0	1	0
d. 12 to 15	120	26	198	28	12	8	39	2
e. 16 to 18	5	1	200	28	17	11	81	5
f. 19 to 25	0	0	115	16	29	18	306	17
g. 26 to 40	0	0	108	15	61	38	580	33
h. 41 to 60	0	0	42	6	29	18	456	26
i. Over 60	0	0	30	4	10	6	304	17
BLANK	4	1	11	2	1	1	9	1
Sex								
Male	189	41	326	46	40	25	360	20
Female	265	57	362	51	111	70	1368	77
BLANK	9	2	21	3	8	5	51	3
National minority group?								
No	84	18	217	30	42	26	587	33
Yes					114	72	1148	65
BLANK					3	2	44	2
IF YES—								
MINORITY RACE								
Negro	322	69	364	51	99	62	1011	57
Spanish-surnamed	46	10	102	14	17	11	140	8
Oriental	0	0	1	0	0	0	7	0
American Indian	1	0	1	0	0	0	11	1
Other	0	0	1	0	0	0	18	1
BLANK	12	3	22	3	43	27	593	33
What type of work do you mostly do or have you done?								
Building trades: carpenter, electrician			22	3	9	6	42	2
Clerical/sales/office/store			148	21	28	18	264	15
Factory worker/mechanic			51	7	26	16	323	18
Hotel/restaurant worker			36	5	11	7	138	8
Janitor/maintenance/laborer			40	6	11	7	96	5
Maid			8	1	6	4	207	12
Nurse			9	1	8	5	40	2
Teacher			19	3	1	1	15	1
Nurse aide/teacher aide/ community aide			44	6	8	5	83	5
Other (Specify)			160	22	26	16	323	18
BLANK			172	24	25	16	249	14

Table 1. (Continued)

	User/CH 465		User 712		User/H 159		Non/Former 1778	
	#	%	#	%	#	%	#	%
Are you presently employed?								
Yes, full-time			137	19	40	25	434	24
Yes, part-time			110	15	11	7	117	7
No			196	28	86	54	997	56
No, in school			228	32	12	8	49	3
No, retired			25	4	8	5	173	10
BLANK			11	2	1	1	10	1
What was the last grade of school you completed?								
1st thru 3rd grade	110	24	7	1	2	1	67	4
4th to 6th grade	321	69	41	6	6	4	200	11
7th to 8th grade	28	6	148	21	15	9	321	18
9th to 11th grade	2	0	261	37	60	38	542	30
Finished high school	1	0	100	14	56	35	464	26
Some college or technical	0	0	76	11	13	8	126	7
Finished college	0	0	54	8	2	1	21	1
Graduate study	0	0	14	2	2	1	13	1
BLANK	3	1	8	1	3	2	26	1
Are you now attending regular school?								
Yes			405	57	24	15	86	5
No			242	34	116	73	1474	83
BLANK			59	8	19	12	219	12
Are you now in any kind of educational or vocational training program?								
Yes			106	15	20	13	80	4
No			543	76	132	83	1638	92
BLANK			58	8	7	4	60	3
How many people in your family are living at home?								
1-3			228	32	51	32	824	46
4-6			282	40	77	48	632	36
7-9			144	20	24	15	237	13
over 9			34	5	6	4	64	4
BLANK			21	3	1	1	23	1
Total weekly income received by all members of your family living at home.								
a. Below $50			46	6	14	9	263	15
b. $50-$99			95	13	30	19	424	24
c. $100-$149			116	16	44	28	393	22
d. $150-$200			137	19	31	19	236	13

Grand Totals

Table 1. (Continued)

	User/CH 465		User 712		User/H 159		Non/Former 1778	
	#	%	#	%	#	%	#	%
e. Over $200 per week			138	19	17	11	127	7
f. Don't know			147	32	19	12	270	15
BLANK			29	4	4	3	67	4
How many blocks is it from the library to where you live?								
Less than one block	34	7	34	5	5	3		
1 to 3 blocks	220	47	158	22	54	34		
4 to 6 blocks	124	27	148	20	33	21		
7 to 9 blocks	27	6	86	12	19	12		
10 to 12 blocks	27	6	76	11	22	4		
13 blocks or over	28	6	211	30	4	3		
BLANK	4	1	2	0	22	14		
How often do you go to the library?								
Once a week or more	331	71	415	58	20	13		
Once a month or more	88	19	173	24	55	35		
Once in six months or more	9	2	40	6	50	31		
Less than once in six months	25	5	78	11	12	8		
BLANK	10	2	4	1	22	14		
When did you start coming to the library?								
First time at library			56	8				
This year			141	20	21	13		
Last year			128	18	34	21		
Within last 4 years			199	28	39	25		
Over 4 years ago			165	23	42	26		
BLANK			22	2	23	14		
Did you use another library before this one?								
Yes			408	57	85	53		
No			222	31	52	33		
BLANK			82	12	22	14		
Do you have a library card?								
Yes	315	68	495	70	79	50		
No	144	31	211	30	56	35		
BLANK	6	1	5	1	23	14		
When did you get it?								
This year	89	19	102	14	9	6		
Last year	84	18	91	13	21	13		
Within the last 4 years	44	9	98	14	20	13		
Over 4 years ago	24	5	202	28	38	24		
BLANK	223	48	217	30	70	44		

Table 1. (Continued)

	User/CH 465		User 712		User/H 159		Non/Former 1778	
	#	%	#	%	#	%	#	%
When you have a few hours of spare time, how do you most enjoy spending it?								
Reading			308	43	63	40	483	27
Talking to friends			85	12	30	19	239	13
Watching television			123	17	45	28	718	40
Listening to records or radio			68	10	16	10	157	9
Do you usually read the newspapers?								
Yes	240	52	588	83	131	82	1462	82
No	163	35	84	12	18	11	225	13
BLANK	61	13	40	6	10	6	86	5
Which do you like to read, magazines or books?								
Magazines	64	14	196	28	42	26	557	31
Books	288	62	263	37	45	28	434	24
Both	43	9	225	32	56	35	414	23
Neither	11	2	10	1	8	5	233	13
BLANK	1	0	2	0	0	0	18	1
	58	12	15	2	8	5	121	7
Did you do any reading last week?								
Yes			643	90	143	90	1329	75
No			59	8	15	9	436	25
BLANK			10	1	1	1	13	1
What did you read?								
Books			502	73	76	48	467	26
Magazines			262	37	63	40	506	28
Newspapers			319	45	89	56	986	55
Other (specify)			30	4	5	3	70	4
Last week, did you watch any TV?								
Yes	434	93	614	86	148	93	2566	88
No	22	5	94	13	11	7	199	11
BLANK	9	2	4	1	0	0	10	1
How many days of the week did you watch TV?								
Every day	350	75	377	53	113	71	1100	62
Weekend only	11	2	27	4	1	1	66	4
1 to 2 days (any others)	14	3	95	23	12	8	116	7
3 to 4 days	29	6	78	11	12	8	199	11
5 to 6 days	28	6	41	6	10	6	109	6
BLANK	33	7	94	13	11	7	188	11

Grand Totals (spanning User, User/H, Non/Former columns)

Table 1. (Continued)

	User/CH 465		User 712		User/H 159		Non/Former 1778	
	#	%	#	%	#	%	#	%
Did you listen to the radio last week?								
Yes	304	65	606	85	121	76	1385	78
No	149	32	104	15	35	22	382	21
BLANK	11	2	2	0	3	2	11	1
WHY CAME TO LIBRARY								
To participate in library program	36	8	44	6	1	1		
To study or get help with school work	146	31	247	35	33	21		
To get job information or books	17	4	50	7	33	21		
To find out about a subject other than jobs	13	3	58	8	30	19		
To get novels for enjoyment	51	11	99	14	46	29		
To bring or pick up children	5	1	23	3	17	11		
To be with friends	59	13	78	11	7	4		
To attend meetings	4	1	6	1	2	1		
To read in library	73	16	123	17	35	22		
To use copying machine	3	1	4	1	8	5		
Other (specify)	88	19	121	17	8	5		
What was your main purpose for going to the library the last time you were there?								
To participate in library program							5	0
To study or get help with school work							70	4
To get job information or books							43	2
To find out about a subject other than jobs							54	3
To get novels for enjoyment							81	5
To bring or pick up children							61	3
To be with friends							9	1
To attend meetings							6	0
To read in library							36	2
To use copying machine							4	0
Other (specify)							0	0
USUALLY GO FOR SAME REASON								
Yes			515	72				
No			171	24				
BLANK			25	4				

Grand Totals

Table 1. (Continued)

	Grand Totals					
	User 712		User/H 159		Non/Former 1778	
	#	%	#	%	#	%
IF NO—						
Why do you usually go to the library?						
(CHECK UP TO 3)						
To participate in library program	9	1				
To study or get help with school work	56	8				
To get job information or books	22	3				
To find out about a subject other than jobs	26	4				
To get novels for enjoyment	42	6				
To bring or pick up children	4	1				
To be with friends	14	2				
To attend meetings	3	0				
To read in library	28	4				
To use copying machine	3	0				
Other (specify)	24	3				
What type of books do you usually read?						
(CHECK ONE)						
Black history, culture	65	9	18	11	118	7
Spanish history, culture	11	2	4	3	21	1
Humor	6	1	3	2	50	3
Love/adventure	78	11	22	14	181	10
Mystery/detective stories	96	13	19	12	148	8
School—related or reference books	74	10	16	10	70	4
Bible	22	3	14	9	207	12
Other (specify)	137	19	17	11	125	7
BLANK	223	31	46	29	858	48
OTHER LEISURE TIME ACTIVITIES						
With my family, children	35	5	14	9	203	11
Sewing, fixing things around the house	40	6	18	11	311	17
Sports, athletics	113	16	11	7	87	5
Go out somewhere	83	12	18	11	136	8

Now I will read you some subjects
that people often want to find out
more about. Stop me when I come
to the ones that would interest
you or your family.

186 *Appendix B*

Table 1. (Continued)

	Grand Totals					
	User		User/H		Non/Former	
	712		159		1778	
	#	%	#	%	#	%
Child care	219	31	62	39	691	39
Household repairs	160	22	50	31	537	30
Medical information or help	281	39	70	44	844	47
Legal help	175	25	54	34	485	27
Birth control	147	21	33	21	305	17
Job information	366	51	77	48	615	35
Racial discrimination	312	44	57	36	506	28
Black/Spanish culture	269	38	47	30	375	21
Sports	298	56	75	47	481	27
Information on money matters	285	40	56	35	562	32

Now I will read you a list of
materials and activities the public
library does have or could have.
Stop me when I come to something
that interests you.

Books, magazines, or						
newspapers	528	74	114	72	1141	64
Movies, records, and tapes	468	66	85	53	737	41
Art exhibits/pictures	373	52	61	38	625	35
Bookmobile	232	33	56	35	489	28
Copying machine	304	43	60	38	436	25
Children's programs	317	45	90	57	908	51
Adult education reading program	348	49	90	57	898	51
Free entertainment, like movies,						
dances, music	471	66	83	52	687	39
Information on job training						
and other services	506	72	100	63	866	49

Now I will read a few statements, please
tell me whether you agree or disagree.
Most people don't go to the library
because nothing's happening there.

Agree	200	28	38	24	350	20
Disagree	479	67	117	74	1241	70
Don't know	26	4	4	3	178	10
BLANK	7	1	0	0	9	1

It's only for people who like to work
or study.

Agree	225	32	53	33	724	41
Disagree	472	66	104	65	985	55
Don't know	7	1	1	1	60	3
BLANK	8	1	1	1	9	1

Table 1. (**Continued**)

	Grand Totals					
	User		User/H		Non/Former	
	712		159		1778	
	#	%	#	%	#	%
It's mostly for people in school, especially kids.						
Agree	195	27	49	31	699	39
Disagree	498	70	107	67	1024	58
Don't know	11	2	3	2	47	3
BLANK	8	1	0	0	8	0
If you've never been inside the building it's probably easy to get lost.						
Agree	112	16	27	17	467	26
Disagree	579	81	124	78	1100	62
Don't know	11	2	8	5	201	11
BLANK	7	1	0	0	10	1
The people who work in the library understand books better than they understand people.						
Agree	173	24	53	33	736	41
Disagree	427	60	87	55	760	43
Don't know	99	14	19	12	271	15
BLANK	9	1	0	0	11	1
It's only for people who can read.						
Agree	43	6	12	8	311	17
Disagree	651	91	142	89	1397	79
Don't know	6	1	4	3	60	3
BLANK	8	1	1	1	10	1
The library is really a place for people who have a lot of free time, not for people who work.						
Agree	115	16	29	18	467	26
Disagree	575	81	128	81	1222	69
Don't know	10	1	2	1	81	5
BLANK	8	1	0	0	8	0
The library's a community organization which tries to make life more pleasant for the people in our neighborhood.						
Agree	624	88	133	84	1537	86
Disagree	66	9	20	13	141	8
Don't know	14	2	5	3	90	5
BLANK	7	1	1	1	10	1
At the library you can find out what to do or where to go if you have a problem.						
Agree	511	72	106	67	1133	64

Table 1. (Continued)

	User/CH 465		User 712		User/H 159		Non/Former 1778	
	#	%	#	%	#	%	#	%
Disagree			154	22	43	27	388	22
Don't know			36	5	9	6	248	14
BLANK			8	1	1	1	9	1
It has programs to help people.								
Agree			572	80	131	82	1275	72
Disagree			51	7	9	6	123	7
Don't know			78	11	19	12	366	21
BLANK			8	1	0	0	14	1
During the past year have you been to a museum?								
Yes	298	64	440	62	59	37	373	21
No	161	35	270	38	97	61	1384	78
BLANK	6	1	2	0	3	2	16	1
During the past year have you been to hear a concert or other live musical program?								
Yes	246	53	445	63	76	48	566	32
No	212	46	263	37	81	51	1206	68
BLANK	6	1	3	0	2	1	6	0
During the past year have you been to an art exhibit?								
Yes	174	37	360	51	53	33	298	17
No	284	61	349	49	103	65	1476	83
BLANK	6	1	3	0	3	2	4	0
How do you usually get to the library?								
Walk	419	90	429	60	86	54	24	1
Bus	12	3	57	8	5	3	2	0
Drive car	2	0	150	21	38	24	5	0
Get a ride in car	25	5	67	9	8	5	3	0
Bike	3	1	2	0	0	0	0	0
Other	1	0	3	0	0	0	0	0
BLANK	3	1	4	1	22	14	1745	98
On this card are different types of programs and services available to people in this area.								
Have you ever heard of the Community Action Agency,_____?								
Yes			393	55	101	64	865	49
No			249	35	58	86	910	51
BLANK			70	10	0	0	2	0

Grand Totals

Table 1. (Continued)

	User 712		User/H 159		Non/Former 1778	
	#	%	#	%	#	%
IF YES—						
How do you know about the Community Action Agency? (CHECK ONE)						
Have been there, used service, visited	79	11	35	22	193	11
Friends, neighbors, relatives, or family	178	25	46	29	408	23
Radio, television, newspaper	84	12	13	8	169	10
Other specify	50	7	7	4	84	5
BLANK	321	45	58	36	924	52
When was the last time you used the Community Action Agency?						
Within last week	29	4	6	4	22	1
Within last month	24	3	6	4	38	2
Within last 6 months	35	5	20	13	64	4
Over 6 months ago	49	7	16	10	129	7
Never/don't know	258	36	52	33	616	35
BLANK	317	45	59	37	909	51
Have you ever heard of the Pre-School Program, _____?						
Yes	458	64	117	74	1130	64
No	184	26	41	26	637	36
BLANK	69	10	1	1	9	1
IF YES—						
How do you know about the Pre-School Program? (CHECK ONE)						
Have been there, used service, visited	51	7	26	16	184	10
Friends, neighbors, relatives, or family	252	35	69	43	657	37
Radio, television, newspaper	91	13	16	10	206	12
Other (specify)	63	9	9	6	88	5
BLANK	255	36	39	25	643	36
When was the last time you used the Pre-School Program?						
Within last week	14	2	6	4	37	2
Within last month	9	1	3	2	21	1
Within last 6 months	15	2	4	3	47	3
Over 6 months ago	42	6	24	15	173	10
Never/don't know	367	52	83	52	863	49
BLANK	265	37	39	25	637	36
Have you ever heard of the Adult Education Program, _____?						
Yes	410	58	115	72	1016	57
No	233	33	43	27	750	43
BLANK	68	10	1	1	10	1

Grand Totals

Table 1. (Continued)

	User 712		User/H 159		Non/Former 1778	
	#	%	#	%	#	%
IF YES—						
How do you know about the Adult Education Program? (CHECK ONE)						
Have been there, used it, visited	72	10	22	14	132	7
Friends, neighbors, relatives, or family	197	28	59	37	576	32
Radio, television, newspaper	57	8	22	14	213	12
Other (specify)	76	11	16	10	89	5
BLANK	310	44	40	25	768	43
When was the last time you used the Adult Education Program?						
Within the last week	40	6	2	1	11	1
Within last month	9	1	3	2	12	1
Within last 6 months	10	1	8	5	25	1
Over 6 months ago	32	4	18	11	117	7
Never/don't know	323	45	88	55	869	49
BLANK	298	42	40	25	744	42
Have you ever heard of the Job Information Center,_____?						
Yes	448	63	112	70	1068	60
No	193	27	46	29	699	39
BLANK	71	10	1	1	7	0
IF YES—						
How do you know about the Job Information Center? (CHECK ONE)						
Have been there, used it, visited	142	20	39	25	240	13
Friends, neighbors, relatives, or family	206	29	57	36	528	30
Radio, television, newspaper	59	8	13	8	204	11
Other (specify)	42	6	3	2	98	6
BLANK	263	37	47	30	708	40
When was the last time you used the Job Information Center?						
Within the last week	22	3	4	3	20	1
Within the last month	31	4	4	3	35	2
Within last 6 months	49	7	21	13	74	4
Over 6 months ago	82	12	20	13	197	11
Never/don't know	260	37	65	41	763	43
BLANK	268	38	45	28	689	39
Have you ever heard of the Public Library,_____						
Yes			155	97	1357	76
No			3	2	411	23
BLANK			1	1	8	0

Table 1. (Continued)

	User/CH 465		Grand Totals User 712		User/H 159		Non/Former 1778	
	#	%	#	%	#	%	#	%
IF YES—								
How do you know about the____library?								
(CHECK ONE)								
Have been there, used it, visited					103	65	382	21
Friends, neighbors, relatives, or family					36	23	725	41
Radio, television, newspaper					5	3	101	6
Other (specify) _____					11	7	148	8
BLANK					4	3	421	24
When was the last time you visited the ____ library?								
Within the last week					30	19	0	0
Within last month					42	26	0	0
Within last 6 months					81	51	0	0
Over 6 months ago					3	2	460	26
Never/don't know					0	0	896	50
BLANK					3	2	422	24
After I read each one, please tell me if you know where you could get information on that subject.								
Child care								
Yes	459	64			83	52	703	40
No	184	26			57	36	873	49
BLANK	69	10			19	12	202	11
Household repairs								
Yes	387	54			63	40	570	32
No	247	35			76	48	1002	56
BLANK	78	11			20	13	205	12
Medical information or help								
Yes	529	74			108	68	1113	63
No	108	15			33	21	464	26
BLANK	75	11			18	11	201	11
Legal help								
Yes	441	62			86	54	825	46
No	198	28			48	30	753	42
BLANK	73	10			25	16	200	11
Birth control								
Yes	399	56			68	43	634	36
No	221	31			69	43	910	51
BLANK	92	13			22	14	234	13
Job information								
Yes	528	74			105	66	876	49
No	113	16			37	23	709	40
BLANK	71	10			17	11	193	11

Table 1. (**Continued**)

	User/CH 465		User 712		Grand Totals User/H 159		Non/Former 1778	
	#	%	#	%	#	%	#	%
Racial discrimination								
Yes			372	52	50	31	369	21
No			278	39	90	57	1201	68
BLANK			62	9	19	12	208	12
Black/Spanish culture								
Yes			434	61	58	36	358	20
No			212	30	79	50	1209	68
BLANK			66	9	22	14	211	12
Sports								
Yes			547	77	95	60	742	42
No			91	13	47	30	821	46
BLANK			73	10	17	11	215	12
Information on money matters								
Yes			352	49	58	36	537	30
No			256	36	77	48	998	56
BLANK			103	14	24	15	243	14
Do you know what kind of things the public library has in it?								
Yes	389	84	639	90	134	84	1116	63
No	58	12	55	8	23	14	646	36
BLANK	18	4	15	2	2	1	15	1
IF YES—								
What are these things?								
Books	381	82	639	90	134	84	1093	61
Magazines and newspapers	125	27	411	58	85	53	647	36
Records and tapes	80	17	258	36	57	36	286	16
Copying machine	28	6	132	19	30	19	104	6
Other (specify) _____	98	21	158	22	25	16	147	8
Do you know what kinds of services and activities the public library has?								
Yes	192	41	365	51	72	45	465	26
No	248	53	310	44	84	53	1265	71
BLANK	25	5	33	5	3	2	47	3
IF YES—								
What are they?								
Tutoring	6	1	53	7	11	7	77	4
Children's programs	104	22	224	31	44	28	353	20
Adult education	6	1	85	12	21	13	107	6
Dances, movies, music	111	24	192	27	32	20	170	10
Other (specify) _____	53	11	128	18	13	8	73	4

Table 1. (**Continued**)

Symbols: User/CH-Children, ages 8 thru 12
User-User, ages 13 and over
User/H-User at home
Non/Former-Nonuser or former user (prior to last 6 months)

The data shown represent totals for fifteen cities, plus, for child users and nonusers, data collected during second site visits to the two pretest cities.

Percentages shown have been calculated separately for each user and nonuser category.

BLANK indicates no response recorded. Coding of nonresponse was done on an earlier data run; the sum of answers to some items may not exactly match grand totals.

separately. The first category is "child users," i.e., children aged eight through twelve. These child users were asked only a portion of the questions in the questionnaire, and they constitute an age group which is *not* represented among nonusers (only nonusers over twelve were interviewed). "Users," i.e., the remaining users interviewed in the branch or program location, constitute the second category. The third category consists of 159 additional users who were interviewed in their homes. Data were collected from 569 individuals classified as users at home, but only the data from 159 questionnaires are shown in table 1. (The balance of these questionnaires were used in the separate subsequent discriminant analysis.) Nonusers (those who have never used the library) and former users (those who used it prior to the last six months) are grouped in a single category. Nonusers constitute about three-fourths, and former users one-fourth of this group.

Analysis of the data shown in table 1 revealed significant differences in age between the user and nonuser populations, which implied that comparisons between these two groups would be of limited value in terms of guiding library program planning. Therefore, a subsequent analysis was done of a subset of these groups: a comparison of adult (thirteen years of age and over) users and nonusers.[1] This analysis involved a comparison of the 569 users at home with the 1,778 nonusers, utilizing the biomedical computer program called "stepwise discriminant analysis."[2] For this analysis a selection of variables was derived from items on the nonuser questionnaire. Table 2 lists the content areas covered by the questionnaire.

[1] See chapter 2 for a discussion of the findings.

[2] W. J. Dixon, ed. *Biomedical Computer Programs* (Los Angeles: Univ. of California Pr., 1967), p.214a.

Table 2. Content Areas Covered by User/Nonuser Questionnaire

Content Area	User Questionnaire Item No.	Nonuser Questionnaire Item No.
Target group		
Age, sex, race	21, 40, 41	21, 40, 41
Grade in school completed	22	22
In school/out of school	23	23
Number in family	24	24
Occupation of subject	37	37
Subject employed	37	37
Income	38	38
Residence in relation to library	28	cover sheet
Use of the library		
History of	30, 31	not asked
Frequency	29	not asked
Possession of card	32	not asked
Knowledge of library resources	18, 19	not asked
Nonuser		
Last time in library	not asked	5
Knowledge of library resources	not asked	18, 19
Former user		
History of	not asked	35, 36
Purposes		
Information needs, various subjects	15	15
Reasons for coming to library	33	35
Modes		
Desire for library materials/ interpersonal services	20, 33	20
Perception of library as not offering interpersonal contact	17	17, 36
Facilities-preference for/against library	17	17, 36
Knowledge of other community agencies	1, 2, 3, 4, 16	1, 2, 3, 4
Convenience of location of library facility	27, 28	
Leisure time activity	6	6
Techniques		
Media		
Reading	10, 11, 14	10, 11, 14
Television	12	12
Radio	13	13
Leisure time	6	6
Subjects of interest		
Library materials, services	20	20
Reading materials	10, 11, 14	10, 11, 14
Television, radio	12, 13	12, 13

Table 2. (Continued)

Content Area	User Questionnaire Item No.	Nonuser Questionnaire Item No.
Leisure time activity	6	6
Cultural events	7, 8, 9	7, 8, 9
Daily life	15	15
Impact measures		
Reasons for attendance	33	
Frequency, duration of attendance (sustained participation)	29, 30, 31, 32	
Perceptions, attitudes toward library	17	17
Preprogram behavior	30, 31, 32	
Postprogram behavior	29, 32, 33	
Knowledge of library materials and resources	18, 19	18, 19

The distribution of these subjects by racial or ethnic groups is as follows:

Ethnic Classification	Users	Nonusers	Total
Nonminority (white)	247	625	872
Spanish surname	113	149	262
Black[3]	209	990	1199
	569	1764[4]	2333

Discriminant analysis enables the assignment of a person to one of the two groups, users and nonusers, through the calculation of the discriminant function. This function·is composed of a set of coefficients, one for each variable. The person's variable value or quantified attribute is multiplied by the appropriate coefficient, the products for all variables are added, and the person is assigned to one group if the result is high and the other if it is low. Although one might expect these coefficients, suitably normalized, to be the measure of the variables, it is hard to ascribe any such meaning to the coefficients. They do not estimate parameters of a statistical model. They are simply the best set of coefficients for discriminating between the two groups in the way described.

[3] Number of users and nonusers classified as black include 8 users and 30 nonusers from other minority groups which it was not feasible to separate for the analysis that follows.

[4] Fourteen of the 1,778 nonuser questionnaires were not used in the discriminant analysis.

A more tangible effect measurement is the F ratio associated with each of the variables in a discriminant analysis. This F ratio is the test statistic for the hypothesis that the distance[5] between the user and nonuser populations is the same whether measured using all variables or all variables but one, the exception being the variable with which the F ratio is associated.

If the significance level associated with the F ratio is too high, i.e., if the F ratio is too small, then the effect of the associated variable may be judged negligible. Significance levels higher than 5 percent or, equivalently,[6] F ratios smaller than 3.84 were taken as negligible.

The significant F ratios thus obtained measure the effect of each of the variables in the analysis. If a new variable is added to the analysis, all the F ratios change. If the analyst knows that the new variable should play a role in any attempt to explain library use, he will hope for a change in F ratios because, in that case, it would represent the adjustment of the old variables' measures to eliminate the new variable's displaced effect. However, the analyst may not be aware of the proper role of the new variable in a study of library use. He may just want to experiment with it. In this situation, he should try it in combination with different subsets of the other variables. Because the total number of subsets is extremely large, a method for selecting and entering variables that chooses some small number of more interesting ones is most appropriate.

The method chosen is as follows:

1. The variable with the largest F ratio when entered singly is chosen at the first step.
2. At the second step, the variable whose F ratio is biggest when entered with the variable chosen at the first step is entered.
3. One variable is entered at each succeeding step. At the nth step the new variable entered is the variable that has the largest F ratio when entered with the $n-1$ variables from the prior steps.

[5] This distance is the population counterpart of the sample distance maximized by the discriminant function. The interested reader is referred to C. R. Rao, *Advanced Statistical Methods in Biometric Research* (New York: Wiley, 1952), p.246ff.

[6] Combined user and nonuser group sizes are so large that ∞ is always a good approximation to the denominator degrees of freedom. The numerator degree of freedom is always one.

4. When all variables or all variables with nonnegligible F ratios are entered, the process stops.

Since simple correlation is an ultimate source of ambiguities in the analysis, the within-group correlations were obtained.[7] A high degree of pre-existing correlation between two or more variables would suggest that the importance of one of these variables might be attributed at least in part to its association with something else. The correlation matrices do in fact indicate high correlations where such would reasonably be expected (between interest in library materials and interest in library services and activities, for example). They also show relatively low correlation among the few variables found to be most significant in discriminating between library users and nonusers, thus supporting the inference that these variables yield independent explanations of library use.

[7] There is just one within-group correlation for each pair of variables, and it is calculated using the variable values from both users and nonusers but in such a way that it is not biased by group differences.